MYSTICAL PRAYER

ISBN: 1717434282 || ISBN-13: 978-1717434289

LOC Control Number: 2018951265

A publication of Tall Pine Books || A division of Pulpit to Page ||PULPITTOPAGE.COM

*Printed in the United States of America

MYSTICAL PRAYER

UNLOCKING THE UNSEEN POWER OF THE HOLY SPIRIT

CHARLIE SHAMP

TALL PINE

ENDORSEMENTS

"There are all of these historical accounts in Christian churches throughout the ages of people caught up in words like "Divine Union" "Trance" and even "Mystical Prayer." What are these and do they have a Biblical basis? Charlie does the most thorough job I have read in modern times of demystifying the mystical without minimizing or trivializing it. I think this is a modern day Fire Within by Theresa of Avila. This will give incredible incentive to everyone whose inner Christian mystic is longing for language and process or examples of how prayer should be the most compelling thing we do in life. So many of these subjects have been taboo or looked at as only experienced by one person in a generation but Charlie creates faith that our connection with God has many tools to activate the kind of relationship Paul talks about in 1 Corinthians 2. From His Spirit he relates His inner most perceptions to ours. For those like me, who have that curious hunger for more connection to God, this will be a refreshing drink to your thirst."

—**SHAWN BOLZ,** Author of *Translating God, Growing Up with God, Modern Prophets*, Host of *Exploring the Prophetic* Podcast, BolzMinistries.com

"My dear friend Charlie Shamp is one of the most prolific apostolic and prophetic voices within our day. This dynamic book centralized around the highest prize in life will radically transform your destiny with great insight, revelation and impartation. It's a *must* read."

—**BRIAN GUERIN**, Founding President, Bridal Glory
International

"In his latest writing, Prophet Charlie Shamp dips deep into the well of revelation and personal encounter to bring a fresh perspective on prayer and intimacy with God. Charlie teaches with cutting edge insight and potent prophetic principles. This writing will challenge you to go deeper and develop a consistent lifestyle of pursuit."

—**RYAN LESTRANGE**, Author of *Hell's Toxic Trio*, Founder
RLM,TRIBE, iHubs & Co-Founder of APB Media

"Charlie Shamp has written a must-read for anyone that desires to go deeper in the Spirit. Mystical Prayer will open you up to prophetic face to face encounters with God and more! This book carries a weight of glory upon the pages of its modern-day revelations, in the same way that Charlie Shamp's ministry carries a tremendous presence of God everywhere that he goes. Read this book – and prepare to unlock the unseen power of the Holy Spirit in your personal life!"

—**JOSHUA MILLS**, Author of *Moving in Glory Realms*,
International Glory Ministries - Palm Springs, California,
JoshuaMills.com

"As the revelation of His GRACE sweeps over the bride and many enjoy freedom, Charlie Shamp reminds us about the importance of relationship, now that we are free. Prayer is simply just that: relating with the Invisible One. It takes one who passionately perseveres the distance to truly value a life of prayer. Like an endurance runner; laying aside all distraction, holding patiently to the promise of the reward no matter how long the journey. The joy of being "still" and waiting on Him, until that dawn begins to break; and He who dwells in unapproachable light presents Himself... Glorious! For the fervent prayer of a righteous man truly does avail much. It's a call for rain in the season of latter rain! This book beckons the reader into a deeper life of prayer... Charlie makes the mystical, both simple and practical. As much as this book is pragmatic it's full of impartation through the wonder-filled life stories related. May you be blessed as you turn the pages."

—**KIRBY DE LANEROLLE**, WOW Life, Sri Lanka

"The book you hold in your hands "Mystical Prayer" by Charlie Shamp has the power to change your life from being a mere nominal Christian to a world changer who lives, moves and manifests the power and glory of the Kingdom of God everywhere you go. I've personally walked with Charlie and Brynn Shamp for many years and consider them a son and daughter in my house. I've also witnessed an insatiable and unquenchable hunger for the manifest power and Presence of God in their lives and have enjoyed many talks with them about the Glory of God. Charlie lives in the secret place of the Presence of Jesus where it's more than just living a lifestyle of contemplative prayer, but he has come know to the great mystic secret of God. The Apostle Paul wrote:

> "...that you may come to know more definitely and accurately that mystic secret of God, which is Christ (the anointed One). In Him all the treasures of divine wisdom and all riches of spiritual knowledge and enlightenment are stored up and hidden." (Colossians 2:2-3 AMP)

Christ is the Great Mystic Secret of God! In this amazing book "Mystical Prayer" Charlie not only unlocks the mysteries of the secrets for breakthrough into the deep things of God, but he provides a blueprint on how to live in this place. I highly encourage you to ingest and digest the amazing truths that are revealed in this book and as you do your life will never be the same! Get ready to be initiated and immersed into the wonderful world of *Mystical Prayer!"*

—**DR. JEFF JANSEN**, Founder of Global Fire Ministries International, Senior leader Global Fire Center Murfreesboro, TN, Author, Revivalist and International Speaker

"God brought Charlie into my life in the year 2000 when I was just 21 years of age. Our comradery, divinely orchestrated by the Lord, has manifested since then into a lifelong living friendship which has inspired and helped shape my own prayer life. From personal experience and traveling around the world with

Charlie, he fully lives every word of this book. Its content will fully unfold, by the spirit of revelation, that there is a deeper prayer life each believer is called to beyond just speaking words to God but allowing God to speak directly to us. This type of prayer is what transformed me and my wife's ministry into bearing great fruit beyond anything I could have ever dreamed through contemplative prayer, night visions, trances, visitations of Jesus, and so much more. All of these are described in this book that the reader can easily understand, seek after, and find in their own lives though hunger. The impartation is real and can be yours throughout the pages of this groundbreaking book. Enjoy and experience it for the rest of your lives and watch Jesus' Kingdom come on earth as it is in Heaven in your life as the greatest harvest of souls in church history is upon us!"

—**MUNDAY MARTIN**, Founder, Contagious Love International, contagiousloveintl.com

"The book of 1 Kings tells the story of the prophet Elijah, a victorious man who moved in power by calling fire down from heaven. He walked in signs and wonders which conflicted the ungodly Queen Jezebel who in turn intimidated Elijah, causing him to flee and hide in a cave. Through all of his chaos, Elijah received a directional word from the Lord for himself, not in the wind, earthquake or fire but by being intimate with his eternal God. That comes with waiting in His presence for the Holy Spirit to release His still voice.

I am impressed with the revelation that God has imparted to

Charlie Shamp while reading *Mystical Prayer.* I believe this to be a most needed prayer guide for the church in this hour. Charlie teaches how patiently and persistently waiting on God enables us to hear, see and decree His kingdom on earth as it is in heaven with signs wonders and miracles.

It is crucial for the body of Christ to walk prophetically in these last days. There is a new breed rising who will walk corporately in the spirit and the power of Elijah to bring the true Word of the Lord for the billion soul harvest. I salute men like Charlie who respond to the roll call of the almighty. He truly is a forerunner of what these end time prophets will look like."

—**ADAM F. THOMPSON**, Prophetic ministry and International Author, voiceoffireministries.org

"If you are looking for Jesus to release His manifest presence through you with signs and wonders, then this is a book you will read and want to re-read. In this book, Mystical Prayer, Charlie Shamp reveals the mystical secrets that most international power ministries are not prepared to share. We are without signs and wonders because much of the Western church has veered from its mystical origins. This is a refreshing read, that molds the miraculous with the mystical. If you have a prophetic gift or want to grow in a prophetic gift and see signs accompany your words, the keys are here."

—**ADRIAN BEALE**, Co-author of *The Divinity Code to*

understanding your dreams and visions, Author, *Hidden in Plain Sight*, everrestministries.com, thedivinitycode.org

"In his new book, Mystical Prayer, Charlie Shamp unlocks supernatural keys to help you come boldly before God's throne of mercy and grace in your prayer life! This is a must read for anyone who wishes to develop an effective and fervent prayer life! I highly recommend this amazing book!"

—**KEVIN BASCONI**, King of Glory Ministries International, Author of *Unlocking the Hidden Mysteries of the Seer Anointing Trilogy*, kingofgloryministries.org

"Mystical Prayer, by Charlie Shamp is guaranteed to make you HUNGRY. You will not be able to read through the pages of this book without pausing to seek God and to press in to encounter Him and His mystical dimension. Mystical Prayer will beckon you to know Him in deeper ways than you ever have before."

—**DR. PATRICIA KING**, Founder of Patricia King Ministries

"Mystical Prayer is one of the most supernatural, practical, and biblical books about encountering God that you will read this year. If you are tired of playing it safe and are ready to experience the radical reality of Jesus, then put all your other books aside and devour this book as quickly as possible."

—**DARREN STOTT**, Pastor Seattle Revival Center

CONTENTS

FOREWORD

One morning I heard a still small voice whisper an important phrase to me, "Quietness is the incubation bed to revelation." When you hear the voice of the Holy Spirit, sometimes you need to let the words sink deeply into you. Other words you hear appear to have a quicker processing chip attached to them and you immediately know or understand what is being stated. But when I heard that phrase, I knew like a cup of hot tea, I was going to have to let this one steep for a while so that the greater meaning and its possible requirements could seep into my heart and soul.

This one phrase altered the course of my devotional walk with God, "Quietness is the incubation bed of revelation." But I had a problem: like many other believers, I let the activity of the beast of my mind dictate what I let my thoughts dwell on and how long I dwelt on them. The resulting impact wasn't good. I had to learn how to "quiet my soul before our God" if "quietness was the incubation bed of revelation." No small task! However, off I went to study, pray, lean in, yearn, wait and eventually learn how to slow my processing chip down long enough to hear the voice of the Lord even in nuances.

Like Charlie Shamp, one of the verses of scripture that became my mentor was Isaiah 40:31. "But those who wait on the Lord shall renew their strength; they shall mount up with wings like eagles, they shall run and not be weary, they shall walk and not faint." But what does it mean to "wait upon the Lord." Now who is the waiter and who is being served? Basic questions rise to the surface when you begin to seek to the Lord to walk a path less traveled – at least in your circles. It is a well-known road for some but for others it is a journey less worn.

Most protestant, evangelical, Spirit-filled Christians, do not have a practical page for what I was about to embark upon. But then I came across a small book by the Dutch Reformed theologian named Andrew Murray called *Waiting on God*. Finally a treasure trove was opened up to me and I started spending hours a day capturing the brilliance of His presence. It was like I had enrolled in a class on "Lessons from the Mystics", and I did not previously even know such a valid class existed. I spent time under the tutorage of the Holy Spirit learning to hear the voice of my Master so much better. I was led into rooms in my Father's House that I did not know existed. Oh to push pause and ask nothing, but to gaze upon the beauty of the Lord and then and only then to inquire in His temple!

So I invite you to go on a journey less traveled with Charlie and Brynn Shamp and myself into Destiny Encounters where *dreams really do come true.* Classes? Oh yes, there are exhilarating new classes to take where the Master truly enrolls you in His School of the Supernatural Ways of God. "Come with Me and you'll see... Come with Me and you'll be... Come and go with Me into an Endless Quest of Mystical Prayer where authentic faith will be born in your heart once again!"

With Anticipation,

—Dr. James W Goll, International Speaker and Author | Founder of God Encounters Ministries | GOLL Ideation LLC

1

CONTEMPLATION PRAYER

A Gaze of Faith... a Silent Love

CONTEMPLATION PRAYER IS A SUBJECT MATTER THAT has often been neglected in the church. In fact, I didn't learn it through reading, listening to teachings, or observing insight from the saints of old. I learned contemplation prayer through *experience*. As I waited in the presence of the Lord, the truths of contemplation prayer became real to me.

His presence is the optimal place of study. See, prayer is more about doing less and *waiting* than it is about trying to make something happen. Prayer is waiting in stillness, not unneeded action.

Many people think that because they are doing a lot, they are somehow accomplishing a lot. That's not necessarily the case. In contemplation prayer, there is a certain stillness... and in that stillness is the power of God. The Bible declares,

"But they that wait upon the Lord shall renew their strength..." (Isaiah 40:31 KJV). Prayer that looks like waiting and stillness is often far more effectual than prayer that looks like striving and unnecessary action.

Even within our charismatic circles and cultures we find ourselves hyped on the adrenaline of vocal, noisy warfare prayer... which has its place. Yet contemplation prayer is much different than this in both form and function. It doesn't require volume or action. It doesn't require noise and effort. It requires something much more still and simple. Later in the chapter we'll unpack in great detail the stages of this type of prayer.

EXPERIENTIAL PRAYER

David said, "My heart and my flesh cry out for the living God" (Psalm 84:2, emphasis added). As we dive into contemplation prayer, I want to make it clear that God Himself comes upon flesh. He comes upon our natural bodies. This is a tangible and experiential reality. Too many have relegated the Christian experience to a merely "spiritual" one and never a *physical* one. This ought not be! I would go so far as to say, it is strange if you do not feel the presence of God in prayer. The Lord wants to come upon your natural body. He wants His presence to be *felt*. There are degrees and levels that He will take you into in contemplation prayer as you come in and wait for Him. "My soul, waits silently for God alone, For my expectation is from Him" (Psalm 62:5).

As you wait upon the Lord in the place of silent stillness, He introduces His peace to you. As you become wrapped in His peace, you begin to dive into deeper levels and places of His presence. His peace is the entry level manifestation, if you will. Suddenly, whether in the body or out of the body, as Paul said, you are caught up in realms and depths of the presence that you didn't know were available.

In that place, prayer becomes a journey and an experience — not a destination. Prayer is no longer a means to an end but an end in itself. In this level of depth you realize that you haven't arrived but you are ever arriving.

People are often trying to end up in a certain place when, in reality, prayer is more about the journey that God has you on. When you realize that we aren't reaching a certain end-place but having an experience, you'll begin to understand that prayer isn't a system or a method. It isn't a well formulated calculation on the part of man but instead it's a fresh experience every time!

When I began to figure this out, I was 18 years old. I would take time to spend with the Lord. I found myself spending hours in the presence of God. Those hours felt like moments. Extended periods of time felt like seconds. I found myself suspended in prayer.

There are places in communion with God in which time

ceases to exist and you can be caught up for hours when it felt as though only minutes went by. This holy suspension is a place to be accessed, not merely fantasized about. God's intention is to bring us into blocked out hours of time in His glory. In so doing, He will impart heavenly realities to us.

We will walk away from those sessions with abilities and graces that we didn't previously have. These hours of stillness will become the most productive parts of your schedule. Suddenly, you find yourself getting more done by basking in the glory than you ever did trying your best to be diligent apart from the presence.

LEARNING FROM THE GREATS

There's a woman of God named Kathryn Kuhlman. God used her as an instrumental tool to spark the charismatic renewal. Watching her flow in the Holy Ghost from the platform was like watching a person completely captivated by Jesus move in sync with His every move. She was a spiritual giant yet spoke with tender love.

Miracles, signs, and wonders were the hallmark of her ministry, and anyone who sat under her could see the genuineness of what she carried. I want to make it clear, however, that her ministry was not the result of a mere gifting, but the result of a deeply committed prayer life. She once said, "God is not looking for golden vessels. God is not looking for silver vessels. God is looking for yielded vessels."

See, God isn't looking for a perfect person, but for a yielded person. As we yield to Him in prayer, God begins to fill our spirit-man with all of heaven. He does this to the point that the very nature of God begins to pour out of our lives. His image and nature become our normal display. I remember hearing wild stories about Kathryn Kuhlman and the way that she exemplified Christ.

At the airport in Pittsburg where she lived, she had her own separate entrance to the airport. Why? Because when she would go places, people would fall out in the Spirit all around her, so they had to create a separation between her and the masses.

Once, she was walking through a hotel and went into the kitchen area and all of the people serving in the kitchen area fell out under the power of God. Such manifestations aren't the result of a random sovereign choice, but an intentional life given to prayer!

Look at Charles Finney, for example. He was in upstate New York and walked into a factory on a typical work day. What happened? Heaven walked in. Everyone in the factory began to weep in the presence of God all at once. Why? Because the man carried a lifestyle of prayer and contemplation prayer. Make no mistake about it, manifestations don't just follow mere gifting... they follow yielded people of prayer.

There was another man by the name of Sundar Singh. He was a mystic from India. They called him "the Apostle of

Bleeding Feet." This was because he walked everywhere without shoes, preaching the gospel. He was heavily persecuted for his ministry.

He was a man of committed prayer and contemplation. He once said, "There are many beautiful things in this world, but pearls can only be discovered in the depths of the sea. If we wish to possess spiritual pearls, we must plunge into the depths. That is, we must pray. We must sink down into the secret depths of contemplation and prayer... and then we shall perceive precious pearls." Sundar also said, "Prayer does not mean asking God for all the things we want. It is rather the desire for God Himself... the only giver of life."

Sundar emanated such a presence of God and carried such an essence of God's Spirit that when he would show up at people's houses, they would mistake him for Jesus. He radiated the very nature of Christ. There are many accounts in which he would knock on the door to someone's house, and they would open the door and think it was an appearance of Christ. People say, "Well, I don't know about that, brother.

Doesn't seem likely." However, it's the will of God in the gospel to craft you into the very image of Jesus. The Lord would like for people to mistake you for Christ. John G. Lake used to wake up in the morning, look in the mirror and say, "Hello, Jesus!"

It might sound crazy and far-fetched, but this is a man who had the bubonic plague die on his hand. When the medical scientists looked up from the microscope and asked how it was possible, he said, "Because the Spirit of God lives in me and the law of the Spirit of life in Christ has freed me from the law of sin and death!" He then moved to Spokane, Washington, to pioneer healing rooms. Within one year of him being there, Spokane was named the healthiest city in all of America. This happened through one man full of God and prayer!

"But those who wait on the Lord shall renew their strength; they shall mount up with wings like eagles, they shall run and not be weary, they shall walk and not faint" (Isaiah 40:31 KJV).

As the verse above says so eloquently, renewal and steadiness are the result of waiting on Him. Too often, we want the mighty manifestations of the great fathers and mothers in the faith, but we don't want to pay the price in prayer! A common theme among these great saints is *contemplation prayer*. They lived, breathed, and practiced contemplation before God. What does contemplation prayer actually look like and how can we attempt it ourselves? Let's break down the basics:

THE FOUR STAGES OF CONTEMPLATION PRAYER:

1) RECOLLECTION

Recollection is an incomplete mystical union or prayer of quiet or supernatural recollection. It's when the action of God is not strong enough to prevent you from distractions, and the imagination still retains a certain liberty. This recollection stage is when you first come into prayer. This is the very first stage of connection with God. Many people never even leave the first stage. It's the place in which we enter His courts with thanksgiving. It's when we release the burdens of the day. In some respects, we are basically unloading on God in this stage of prayer.

In this place, we often tell the Lord about the issues and struggles. We ask God for help with ourselves, with people, with family, with circumstances, and so forth. This place is a switching over from the busyness of life to the stillness of prayer. If you're baptized in the Holy Ghost, it's often a place where we simply pray in tongues and begin to enter in.

Recollection is a place in which we start to get our feet wet in His presence, as it were. We are climbing over the hurdles of the day in this place. It's a very, very necessary stage... yet it isn't the *only* stage. If prayer were a house, recollection would be the foyer. In recollection, our mind still wanders. We are praying, yet we still wander mentally to natural things and other life issues. Perhaps we find ourselves checking our phones and wondering if so and so will respond to us soon or what the score of the big game is.

I've personally learned to not take my phone into the prayer room. If people need to get ahold of me, the world won't end if I respond after prayer. Some think that prayer takes away from caring for natural things. However, I've found that the more I pray, the more I actually get done for God. Productivity actually increases as prayer increases. Some think that their schedule will be sacrificed if they increase prayer and as a result they'll accomplish less. The inverse is actually true. If prayer decreases, the schedule is packed with works and effort that lead to a less accomplished life!

The mind in recollection is sorting through the transition from work, life, and everything else to the sweetness of communion. It might take you some time to get all of that stuff off of you. It could take thirty minutes or even an hour. If it takes longer, it takes longer — but the press-through is worth it!

You know, most Christians quit praying as soon as they feel that burden lift off of them. They walk out of prayer before coming into the second stage, let alone the third and fourth. As soon as God's peace comes and they feel a release, they say, "Hallelujah, that was prayer. I'm good." The problem is, prayer is less about us talking and more about God talking to us.

If we will incline our ears and press into a further experience, we'll find the riches of God being released to us in new ways. Don't you know that God is a rewarder? The measure of the reward can sometimes be determined by the measure of pressing in that is done on our parts.

 Prayer is less about us talking and more about God talking to us.

2) MEDITATION

Some folks say, "Oh, my. Meditation is demonic. That can't be of God." Here's my question: do you think Satan created anything? Or do you think he just perverted it? Of course, he perverted it. He has perverted true biblical mediation, yet this doesn't mean we should cast off the authentic practice! Don't make the mistake of throwing the baby out with the bath water. Don't toss out a rich practice because of a false version of it that happens to exist.

This second stage is where the soul begins to focus on heaven. Meditation is a full or semi-ecstatic union. The mind becomes renewed. You've walked through the gate. You've already passed into a place in which God and His Word are alive to you. This is a place in which the strength of the divine action keeps the person fully occupied, but the senses can continue to act, therefore, by the will of the person, they can cease prayer, if they'd like. You aren't yet overcome in this place but you're yielding more and more of your triune being to the presence of the Lord.

This is the stage in which the mind comes into peace and gets renewed by the Word. You start stepping into the inner court or the holy place, or the lamp stand of God. In this, your mind is illuminated. You begin to partake of the show-bread and the table of incense. Intercession begins to rise up within you.

What you find in studying the order of the construction of

the tabernacle and its components is quite interesting and meaningful. The types and shadows are profound! See, God first told Moses to make the Arc of the Covenant, which represented the glory of Christ Jesus.

The second piece was the showbread, which represented God's glory being manifest in our domestic realm here on earth through His incarnation. The showbread was a physical, earthly representation of the glory of God. Jesus came as an earthly manifestation of the heavenly Father. He is our showbread, if you will. He is the bread of heaven which we can partake of.

As these things are consumed, you are stepping into deeper places. Your soul starts to quiet and come into rest in this stage. Are you beginning to grasp the levels and depths of contemplation prayer? In this place, you're eating of the presence of God. Thoughts of the day start to leave and scriptures become illuminated.

This is the place where your strength starts to renew. Many believers are weary and fainting because they aren't entering the holy place! They aren't going beyond the gate and into the courts! They are just casting off burdens without coming into the place in which they sup with the King. See, in this place of communion, we draw so close to the Father, Son, and Holy Spirit in such a way that the cares and concerns of this world begin to fade. Weights lift and your spirit becomes light with tranquility.

The Scriptures become alive and revelation starts to come.

Your posture of prayer and meditation attracts insight and revelation to you. It isn't because you're reading the Word, but because you're eating the Word. God sets up His lamp stand within you. Suddenly, the scriptures that you didn't understand are absolutely comprehendible.

Samuel, for example, would actually lay at the lamp of God. The Bible says there was no widespread revelation at that time. Yet Samuel would enter into contemplation by laying by the lamp and meditating on the Lord. In that time, God suddenly began to speak.

See, it's lying next to the lamp stand, so to speak, that triggers a release of revelation and insight into the very Word and voice of God. In that story, God spoke, but Samuel didn't recognize it at first. Why? Because he wasn't trained. Eli knew principles, but not the presence. It's a mistake to know principles but not the presence.

At first, he didn't instruct Samuel properly. However, a third time became the charm as Eli caught on and then instructed Samuel to listen to the voice of the Lord. In that place of response, revelation began to flow, and thus, a prophetic ministry was launched that absolutely changed the world, both then and now.

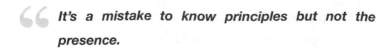 *It's a mistake to know principles but not the presence.*

See, I often position myself to lay before God on the floor. I'll just start to ask the Holy Spirit to come and bring illumination. I begin to pass in and through the stages of contemplation prayer. In this, there is an expanse that begins to take place. It feels like the room even begins to expand. You feel as though you're being lifted. Angels come and lift you into the presence of God. These are the precious byproducts of meditation.

3) UNION

This is an ecstatic union. The root word of ecstatic being ecstasy. This is when communication with the external realm (or the world) are severed, or nearly so, and no one can bother you. You can no longer move or be moved from that state. Let me tell you, when you enter this stage, you will feel like your body is expanding, in a sense.

You'll start to feel as though you cannot move. A holy heaviness of the Holy Spirit will begin to come upon you. The word glory in the Bible is described as a person or a thing of heaviness. Not a negative heaviness, but a healthy heaviness. In this state, your body loses its ability to move.

You may even feel a sense of numbness. This happens from the top of your head to the soles of your feet. Some experience this in meetings, actually. I was just recently in meetings in another nation and we did an anointing service for kids from 5 years old to 18.

As I prayed for them, the power of God would touch them. I

left the meeting with people still laying on the floor laughing, weeping, and speaking in tongues. Four hours later, I got a picture message from the pastor. People were still laid out on the floor and ushers had to pick them up and carry them out of the meeting. Kids weren't coming out of the Spirit. They were suspended between heaven and earth. In this precious arena, you're wholly at the mercy and control of the Spirit.

Sadly, folks experience such things in meetings, but they don't in their own prayer times. See, you can only release such glory on others if you carry it. If you spend time in this place of communion and ecstasy, you'll carry an ability to release the supernatural to a degree that others don't.

In union, the lines between natural and supernatural become blurry. You're still in your body, but your body is no longer active. What is happening is your soul and your spirit are becoming separated.

Like in Hebrews 4, the spirit and soul are being divided by the Word. In this third place of union, you're being overcome by the presence of God. You aren't working the presence. You aren't coercing it. He is there!

4) ECSTASY

When you study out the scriptures, you see examples of this. In the book of Acts, Peter was in a trance and saw a vision of animals that came down and he heard from God. The word trance in this passage is actually the Greek word ekstasis.

This is the stage in which you begin to blend and marry into God. You know, a bride doesn't have any rights with the husband or enjoy any benefits of the marriage until the consummation of the union. Once the union takes place, the wife has full access to everything contained in the marriage covenant. God wants to marry us. We are His bride. We have a union with Him. There will be a day in which we will have a marriage supper and an ultimate consummation.

Yet, there is a place in prayer of *marriage with God*. It's the ecstasy of prayer! You become so wrapped up in Him that there is a meshing of heaven and earth. There is a divine blending between the spirit of man and the Spirit of God. Oneness is achieved in this place. You're past closeness and nearness. You are now jelled together with the Lord, so to speak.

"I know a man in Christ who fourteen years ago—whether in the body I do not know, or whether out of the body I do not know, God knows—such a one was caught up to the third heaven" (2 Corinthians 12:2).

Paul was caught up in a place of ekstasis. A marriage in the spirit between God and the person. A blending of realms in which you don't know if you're in your body or not! In this place, God showed Paul secrets and intimate things that Paul couldn't even speak of! God doesn't share intimacy with everyone... but He wants to. In fact, the Bible says that God wanted to have an intimate relationship with an entire nation. He created mankind as a whole for intimacy.

He formed Israel and had a heart that said, "I want to marry you. I want to be intimate with you." Yet Israel chose comfort and safety over marriage with God. Why? Because of fear. They saw the mountain that burned with fire and refused. They sent Moses instead of going themselves.

God chose Israel for intimacy, but Israel chose distance for safety. Did you know that presence is the most prominent feature of heaven? Heaven is heaven because of the presence of God.

The depths of intimacy with the glory of God is our call, here on earth as it is in heaven. In your own personal life, what value do you place on the presence of God? Most ministers love to minister to people when, really, their first call is to minister to the Lord. God separated to Himself an entire tribe called Levi to stand in a place of ministry to Him!

 Most ministers love to minister to people when, really, their first call is to minister to the Lord.

God desires ministry unto Himself. Oh, that the church would understand how God is longing for fellowship and intimacy with people. The veil that separated God from people was six inches thick. There were no stitches or loose pieces of tapestry. Yet the priests would go through the veil. How? Only by supernatural means.

Oh, that we would understand that entering God's presence

requires supernatural experience! That we would pass from recollection and into meditation... and that we would jump deeper into a sold out union and eventually into the majestic place of ecstasy with God.

Many people never actually experience the true life of God. They instead stay in the outer courts, missing out on the tremendous blessing of total intimacy with God. When was the last time you had pillow time with the Lord? If you're married, you know the beauty of laying with your spouse and simply talking or whispering.

When did you last enjoy sweet intimacy with the Lord in which you allowed Him to whisper to you? These things don't happen overnight, but it's accomplished through cultivating a lifestyle of prayer and intimacy.

Esther was waiting for months before coming into covenant with the king. She had to be prepared and readied. Let me ask you, what if you spent six months in prayer as preparation for just one night of encounter with the glorious presence of God?

This is the life. This is the place that God brands you. It's the place where He begins to marry you. It's the place that you're marked irreversibly. The glorious encounter He gives you is so exceedingly worth the time spent in contemplation and prayer.

"He who dwells in the secret place of the Most High shall abide under the shadow of the Almighty" (Psalm 91:1). To abide under the shadow of the almighty is to come under the canopy of God. What is this canopy? See, when a Jewish couple get married, they do so under what's called a huppah. It's a canopy. The huppah represents a covenant that they're entering into. The shadow of the Almighty is the huppah, the canopy, the cloud of His presence. In this, you're standing under the covenant and marrying/being married to God Himself.

Let Him enwrap you with His glory and love. Step into His gates, and don't fear His courts. Dive into the Holy of Holies and never void the deeper places. In fact, let your longing for the depths of God inspire you to travel in and through these precious stages of contemplation. The fruit that such living yields is far beyond what is common to man. Yet it can be yours through earnest prayers of contemplation.

2

THE PRAYER OF THE MYSTIC

Decoding the Saints of Old...

THE PRAYER OF THE MYSTIC ISN'T ANYTHING NEW. IN fact, it has been around for a very long time. It is fairly new, however, to the Pentecostal and Charismatic movement. When we think of praying, we often think of praying in tongues. For some, praying in their understanding and praying in the Spirit are the only two facets of prayer that they understand or are familiar with. However, there's more to prayer than these two faculties alone.

Old time Christian mystics taught on prayer, yet their language can be difficult to understand and decode because of the time period in which they lived. The reading can be quite heavy. I'd like to take some time in this chapter decoding and unwrapping the truths of this subject.

FRIENDSHIP WITH HOLY SPIRIT

"The grace of the Lord Jesus Christ, and the love of God, and the communion of the Holy Spirit be with you all. Amen" (2 Corinthians 13:14, emphasis added). The Apostle Paul was a forerunner during his time in explaining and expounding upon mystical experiences with the Holy Spirit. He often used the words fellowship and communion to describe his interactions with the unseen realm. Over and over again throughout the epistles you can see him trying to convey this message to those he was connected with in the spirit. That there was a higher realm of relationship one could posses with the Holy Spirit.

There is a place of prayer where you begin to be submerged into His presence. In that place, God starts to speak to you, as we've discussed. Please note, it isn't a mere verbal communication, but one that is spirit to Spirit. The Greek word for communion in the verse above is koinonea. The word koinonea means six things. They are:

1. Presence
2. Fellowship
3. The sharing of one's self
4. Participation
5. Intimacy
6. Communion

That is what the Spirit of God desires to have with you. These things begin to happen when the Holy Spirit has *friendship* with you. There becomes an exchange of presence. There's fellowship and friendly communication. God begins to share Himself with you and you with Him. As He does, He isn't hands-off, but completely hands-on with His participation. Intimacy is cultivated, which is the goal of prayer. See, the kingdom is all about intimacy. It's more about what you *feel* than it is what you *see*. Everyone is wanting to see things in prayer. Yet, when we dive into this realm, we feel Him and experience Him sometimes before we start seeing visions and so forth.

Frustration comes in prayer because we often expect the heavens to open and we suddenly start talking with Christ face-to-face after five minutes of prayer. This shouldn't be. Practice makes perfect. Prayer is something to be practiced. Kathryn Kuhlman used to say that she would practice the presence of God. As you do, you'll start to climb higher in the things of God and prayer.

As we climb in prayer, it's quite common for thoughts contrary to God and His Word to infiltrate. What's required on our part? Simply subject those thoughts to the character of God and continue to press past the mire of wrong thinking. Distraction will try to delay you from pressing in. Consider the old time mystics who entered great depths in God. Did those mystics experience distraction? Of course. Did they have to push past the cares of their day? Of course.

They were not exempt from these things; they are like you and me. The call to continue in Him is ever remaining. Never make the mistake of thinking that someone else is able to reach high places in prayer because of a special grace or a proprietary gifting. No! They are required to hop aboard the same pursuit that anybody and everybody is.

THE SECRECY OF ENCOUNTERS

As we unpacked earlier, Paul pushed in and reached such great heights in God. He was caught into the third heaven, a place of ecstasy. When describing this, he made a very interesting statement that I want to draw your attention to: "And I know such a man—whether in the body or out of the body I do not know, God knows— how he was caught up into Paradise and heard inexpressible words, which it is not lawful for a man to utter" (2 Corinthians 12:3-4, emphasis added).

There are things that happen within the prayer of the mystics that you cannot even utter to man. When you live from encounter to encounter, I want you to know that there are certain things that will happen to you that God won't even permit you to share with another. Why? Because the Lord is marrying you... and if you're married, you know there are certain things that happen between husbands and wives emotionally, physically, and spiritually that is for them only. Things that only they have access to know.

There are times that I go to share about an encounter I've had with the Lord and I feel an urge to pull back because there is almost a sensitivity in the subject. One of the issues in having a culture of sharing about encounters so openly and so frequently is we can fall into the trap of trying to one-up each other's encounters. We get into comparison and, as a result, we feel like we don't measure up to the other folk's encounter.

Then suddenly, we attempt to strive to get into the next realm. When in reality, none of this works through striving. Comparison will never produce a deeper walk with the Lord. Don't take a private encounter with the Lord and spill it with the crowd for pats on the back and ooh's and ahh's! Cherish the intimate fellowship and share moments when you're led to do so. Shake off the condemnation trap of comparison and rest in what you have in Jesus.

When you begin to have encounters with the Lord Jesus, you may see, hear, and experience things that take you months or even years to compute. I've had times where I've seen something that I didn't understand and I've had to just put it on the shelf for a while. For example, people think that all angels look like Fabio's or little cherubs with harps. However, we see in Ezekiel or Isaiah where they're seeing creatures with teeth, faces, or even lion-like countenances.

In this realm of seeing, the possibilities are endless. It might not make sense in the moment. Your job isn't to necessarily explain or direct it all. Shelf what needs to be shelved and figure out what needs to be figured out. But never, never compare it to everyone else's experience and try to figure out where you stack up.

I don't want to merely explain what these deep places in God are like, but I want to lay grid-work for actually getting there. In the aforementioned stages of contemplation prayer, it's important to note that as you practice these things, you'll become quicker at climbing through these stages. You'll become quicker at shaking off burdens and entering His peace, His meditation, and eventually ecstasy. As you do, I want to note that it's important that you don't become discouraged if you aren't reaching the deeper stages every time right away. Don't forget that it's a journey, not a destination.

THE WAY

"And whither I go ye know, and the way ye know. Thomas saith unto him, 'Lord, we know not whither thou goest; and how can we know the way?' Jesus saith unto him, 'I am the way, the truth, and the life: no man cometh unto the Father, but by me'" (John 14:4-6 KJV).

Jesus is actually the tabernacle of God. He is the doorway by which we enter God's presence. In the natural tabernacle, there were three realms: the outer court, the inner court, and the holy of holies. The initial gate in the tabernacle was called "the way." After that, you came into the holy place, which was called "the truth." Finally, the priest would go through the veil. He didn't go around it, under it, or over it. He went through it, and that place was called the holy of holies. He went through it, into the Holy of holies, which was called "the Life." In the holy of holies, blood was sprinkled on the mercy seat.

Over the mercy seat, two angels touched. The Shekinah glory would come and it wasn't merely a flame as some might think. In fact, a portal would open. The arc was a transportation device. First Chronicles and Ezekiel both talk about these concepts in more detail. They mention a wheel within a wheel and the chariot of the cherubim. As the wheel would begin turning, the priest would go into the portal of the arc.

He would go into the portal and race through the dimensions of time and space and grab the blood of the Lamb from the foundations of the world and apply it as atonement for the people. The Lamb was slain from the foundations of the world. It's an eternal concept. The reason that Jesus had to come into time was because time didn't know that He died. So, for everyone to get in on the fullness of the sacrifice, He had to come into the space of time for everyone to experience and obtain His sacrifice. The priests of old, however, could dip into this dimension and cash in on a sacrifice that wasn't yet available to the masses.

As we take in these concepts, just know that every Old Testament symbol and type has a New Covenant application. There are five stages in the contemplative, mystical prayer realm I want to unfold to you:

---

1) THE OUTER COURTS (THE WAY)

This is where Jesus becomes real. If you climb up any other way, you're a thief and a robber, according to the scriptures. See, when witches and warlocks dive into the spirit realm apart from Christ Jesus, a part of them dies. Witches and warlocks trade on human or animal sacrifices. But see, we trade on the blood of Jesus. We enter the spirit realm covered in the precious blood of Jesus.

2) THE INNER COURT (THE TRUTH)

As you go through the place of the inner court, your mind is renewed and illuminated. In the inner court is the lamp stand. As we've unpacked, the lamp stand illuminates something that you could not see without it. This is the holy place. This is the place of prayer in which you begin to see things and access things that weren't accessed and seen before.

The illumination of the Word is a very underestimated facet of prayer. See, the Word being illuminated to you is actually the way in which you access the holy of holies. It is the means by which we go deeper... or the key to unlock the next phase.

3) THE TABLE OF SHOWBREAD

The table of showbread was the second item developed for the tabernacle. It is the glory of God from the holy of holies made available in the natural, so to speak. It's the bread that we partake of. It's representative of the fullness of God.

The showbread is a display of God in a very natural, practical way. It's a table overlaid in gold. It points to Christ coming as the golden glory of heaven, yet taking on very natural, practical flesh to be available to humanity... not just for our amazement, but for our feasting! We are to partake of Christ's very flesh and Christ's very being.

4) INTERCESSION

The table of incense was a part of the inner courts. Incense was as intercession going up and entering the nostrils of God as a sweet smelling aroma. When we pray in an unknown tongue, the Bible says we speak mysteries to God. Tongues are such a beautiful means of intercession because it's a prayer that only God Himself can decode!

"For he that speaketh in an unknown tongue speaketh not unto men, but unto God, howbeit i n the spirit he speaketh mysteries." (1 Corinthians 14:2 KJV)

For the believer, tongues are a direct line that takes our communication out of natural human language and brings it into a heart-to-heart encounter with God: Spirit talk. The question then becomes, what are the mysteries of God?

In the Amplified Bible, 1 Corinthians 2:10 calls them the deep and bottomless things. Paul uses a unique Greek word to describe this mysterious communication, mysterion. This word can also be translated as sacrament in English, which gives us an understanding of feasting upon Christ.

The word literally means the secret counsels which govern God in dealing with the righteous, which are hidden from ungodly and wicked men but plain to the godly. There are all kinds are hidden treasures in Christ and we have the ability to tap into those mysteries by praying in tongues. There are mysteries about God Himself that by praying in the Spirit, we uncover. Also by this practice we uncover mysteries about the realm of the spirit as well as events that have yet to take place in the natural world. Mysteries in areas of technology, entertainment, science, politics, and the creative arts.

We are shown not only what is to come in the future, but what the Lord want us to do with it. All of these things are waiting to be given birth to through those who will give themselves to praying in tongues. As we pray these hidden mysteries, they go up into the realm of the spirit as sealed documents... classified information, you could say. As the Lord receives them He breathes these communications in

and exhales the answers. They come in the form of Apoka-
lypsis or Revelation and what was previously unknown
becomes revealed!

You can truly get stuck in this place of intercession. Paul
described it as groaning that can't be uttered. It's something
more than warfare tongues. It's a deep, deep groaning of
intercession. God breathes in these prayers. He breathes in
this worship.

5) THE HOLY OF HOLIES (THE LIFE)

This is the place where you partake of the glory. You start to
experience Him directly. The first thing you see in this place
is light. It's as if the eye of God looks over you. Instead of
looking at the light, go through it. In that place, you'll enter
new dimensions. You actually begin to see things in this
place. It's almost as if a tunnel comes and carries you. In this
dimension, you may start to hear angels.

Let me share one experience with you. I was in this place of
prayer. In the spirit, I was taken up and brought to a door.
Now, I have a master's degree in theology, but I don't have a
theological grid-work for this experience.

As I came to this gigantic door, I walked up these steps. As I
did, the door opened and I met a child. The child looked like
me. I was so shocked and dumbfounded. It was too much for
me. I felt myself go back into myself. I said, "God, what was
that?"

I didn't recognize until years later that I actually met my son in heaven. When my wife became pregnant with our first child, I said, "It's going to be a boy" and I told her his name. I knew this because I'd already seen him. Of course, these things came to pass. See, at the time of the encounter, I wasn't married and hadn't even met my wife. Sometimes, the revelation behind an encounter isn't brought to light until later.

These stages of prayer and experience are the ultimate illuminators in many, many ways. For example, before I began entering this deep realm, I didn't like science. I flunked it as a kid. However, now I teach on quantum physics and I love it!

In January 2014 I was on a quest to seek after the deeper things of God. Day and night I was waiting upon God in prayer for a visitation. After nearly fourteen days of locking myself in, I had a visitation. The room became electrified with the presence of God and suddenly an angel manifested. This Angel grabbed me by the hand and it felt as if two hundred volts of electricity were flowing through my body, I began to shake uncontrollably. At the same time knowledge began to flood my mind. I understood things about science and creation that I could never understand before. I saw how God created things through words and sound. I understand how quantum physics and the glory of God worked on simpler planes. A total supernatural download had taken place in the spirit. Later that year I found myself by God's direction in an Asian nation meeting with the top quantum physicists to discuss what heaven had revealed to me by revelation. Only God could make such things happen.

I have found that in deep places of prayer, God opens the mind to understand and quantify what you couldn't before. Allow yourself to be immersed in these places. Let the journey captivate you. Put aside preconceived notions about prayer and pick up the truth of the depths that are available. Let God encounter you, as you encounter Him.

THE FOUR DIMENSIONS OF SEEING

Encounters of a Heavenly Kind...

JOHN G. LAKE WAS ONCE IN A MEETING MINISTERING. He was taken up and came down in a hospital room where a man was sick, thousands of miles away. Lake prayed for the man and he was healed. He then was transported back to the meeting in an instant. God transported him through the spirit realm, through the place Lake called "the lightnings of God."

This wasn't the only time this happened to Lake. Once while in a prayer meeting He knelt to intercede and saw the lightning come and again was taken in the Spirit to an insane asylum where he laid his hands upon a woman and cast the devil out of her. He returned to the prayer meeting to tell of what he had seen and experienced. Many thought he was crazy until several weeks later they received a letter confirming that Lake had indeed been seen at the insane asylum praying for the woman and she was now free and in her right mind!

How was this possible? Lake and any other born-again Christian live and move and have their beings in Him. Therefore, we aren't limited to earthly means of transport. We are seated with Christ in heavenly places. This means we dwell outside of time and space. You can move beyond where you are in time and space through these openings in the spirit.

When you enter this realm in the spirit, your body never leaves the earth... you just shift worlds. The more you practice moving in the realm of the spirit, the more real it becomes to you. With some, the struggle has been understanding the process of going fully into that dimension.

Often, people feel like the place that they are in prayer isn't fully where they feel they belong in the spirit. People think, "Well, if the kingdom is coming into these deep places and I'm not in it, then I must not be a part of it." That is wrong thinking. Give yourself grace in these areas. We must begin to walk like Enoch. Enoch walked with God for 365 years and then God took him. Enoch started walking with God by faith. Notice this word *faith*... because it is key.

The Bible does not say it was by Enoch's personal anointing that he was translated nor does it say it was by the glory. He wasn't translated because he carried a special grace or even because he knew something that others didn't. The Bible states that he did it all by *faith*. Everything that we do starts by faith and believing. It's the key that unlocks everything. The Bible discusses this in great detail in Hebrews 11.

Perhaps the first day or the first year, Enoch saw very little or felt very little. Finally, in the last year of Enoch's life on earth, God sort of said, "You've taken on too much of heaven. You've got to come here for good." Enoch probably had less understanding than you have as a New Testament believer. Imagine what's possible for you today!

Some think that when they die, they'll start to experience heaven and encounter the heavenly realms. In this, death has become their savior and their door of access to the supernatural dimension. This isn't what is taught in the gospels. As we read earlier, Jesus is the door! He is the pathway into the supernatural. In all actuality, we rob God from blessing us when we don't pass through the door of Christ into the spirit realm. A door is a glory portal. A glory portal is a supernatural structure in space-time manifested as a long, thin tunnel connecting points that are separated in space and time.

SEEING

For some people, they get caught up in comparison and struggle with seeing in the spirit. With eyes fixed on everyone else's encounter, you'll struggle to see for yourself what God wants to do. Enoch was different than Elijah, but they both rode the chariot.

Be you, in Him... not someone else. You have a specific breath of God within your specific being, different from anyone else. Allow the uniqueness of your relationship with Jesus to be more and more real to you.

There are four realms of seeing in the spirit which we must look into. The last thing we should do is relegate communication with God to sounds or feelings. There are things to see and visions to behold.

 Enoch was different than Elijah, but they both rode the chariot.

1) THE DIVINE COMMUNICATION

It's the Hebrew word chazown. It's simply communication between you and God. In this place, there is more sound than there is sight. A supreme blessing of this place is the renewing of the mind that takes place here. We have to understand, there is a difference between your brain and your mind.

I ask people in meetings to touch their mind, and most of the time, the group as a whole puts their hands on their head. Yet, the mind isn't the brain. The brain is a natural muscle, but the mind is something attached to our spirits. Paul said, "and be renewed in the spirit of your mind" (Ephesians 4:23, emphasis added).

Why is all of that important to us? Because our minds are

able to transcend time and space and enter the spirit realm of God. They aren't limited to a natural brain or earthly function. As dialogue between God and man takes place, our minds are maintained in God and we are positioned to receive the Word of God. It's God building an infrastructure within our minds to receive the implanted Word of God.

Prophets of old would go into visions, but the Hebrew word for vision was chazown. It describes not necessarily the audible voice of God, but a spirit-to-spirit communication between them and the Lord. As they would hear the Word, they would speak the Word and frame up the world. They would begin to align their spirit with that dimension.

Observing and understanding these ways which the prophets of old saw, will enable us to see in a similar fashion. You will always duplicate the things you study and unpack the most.

Don't allow your prayer times to fall short of chazown. Don't quit prayer before you enter the place of divine communication. When the Word of God begins to illuminate, and you're doing less talking and more contemplating, don't stop, but let your spirit slip into communication with God. In this place, it isn't about words back and forth; it's about a wordless, spirit-to-spirit communication.

Even from person to person on a human scale, we can experience this wordless communication. It's a fellowship of spirits that takes place. With some people, you just have an instant connection. There is a communication that goes beyond words that only God can arrange and align. This sweet connection isn't merely horizontal, but vertical between us and the Father.

See, after being born into this world, we had to learn communication. We had to learn the ins and outs, the "dos" and the "don'ts." That being the case, how much more we have to learn now that we've entered a realm of divine communication with a heavenly Father.

Nicodemus met with Jesus in secret and exchanged interesting dialog:

"There was a man of the Pharisees named Nicodemus, a ruler of the Jews. This man came to Jesus by night and said to Him, 'Rabbi, we know that You are a teacher come from God; for no one can do these signs that You do unless God is with him.' Jesus answered and said to him, 'Most assuredly, I say to you, unless one is born again, he cannot see the kingdom of God'" (John 3:1-3).

Notice, Jesus said unless you're born again, you cannot see the kingdom of God. In other words, unless you've been saved, you cannot become exposed to the visual realm of beholding the kingdom.

This born-again experience enables us to witness what God is doing in the spirit. Don't shortcut your spiritual education, so to speak, but allow yourself to explore the kingdom and the realm you've been born-again into!

GROWING UP IN THE SPIRIT

In the natural, when a baby is born, the doctor will slap the baby because the baby doesn't know how to breathe. It's never been into that dimension before. The doctor gives it a smack. Is the doctor mean? No! It's saving the baby's life. Suddenly, the baby starts to breathe and it cries. It didn't understand breathing air up until that point because it was in a different dimension before. Then the baby grows, learns to walk, talk, communicate, and be productive.

It's the same way in the spirit realm! Don't worry about where you are in the spirit age-wise. Simply allow God to take you along in the growth process. God will jolt you to wake you to new concepts and realms!

He will encounter you and introduce new places to you and from that place, you'll begin to step forward into various places of growth and development.

Let me paint another picture for you. I love fishing. Fish love swimming. They only understand one dimension. That's swimming in water front, back, and side to side. If I catch that fish, it will experience a dimension that it didn't understand before. Suddenly, it's out of its normal dimension, and starts feeling air and seeing trees, people, birds, and grass. Out of its normal dimension, it doesn't know how to breathe or function.

Likewise, people seeking spiritual experiences outside of a born-again experience will be like fish out of water — experiencing a realm that they weren't wired to experience. However, through a salvation experience, we become new creatures that are equipped and ready to experience the riches of new realms in the spirit. That realm is your inheritance. It's what Jesus paid for.

Folks who are in the occult can experience the spirit realm. Born-again Christians are called to experience the spirit realm. The difference is the access point.

There has been in recent years a re-emergence of certain ancient occult practices that at one time were marginalized, to a larger extent, only to those privy to hallucinogenic drug use in Amazonian Shamanic ceremonies. These shamanic rituals in the Amazon are now growing in popularity across the world. Dimethyltryptamine, or DMT, is the active ingredient in ayahuasca, which is a plant-based mixture that can be smoked to give users a hallucinatory 'journey' more extreme than that of LSD, ketamine or magic mushrooms.

Within minutes of taking this plant-based substance the user is whisked away into another dimension. Most users find it hard to describe their experiences once returning to a normal consciousness, but all have undoubtedly come back speaking of having interactions with alien entities that teach them higher realms of knowledge.

These interactions are leading many who have experienced these altered states of consciousness to continue to take DMT to learn more from these entities about life.

These "spirit guides" often show the user beautiful things that have no human language to describe and talk with them on a plane of reality beyond human words. Speaking to them about existence beyond the three-dimensional world that we live in and various topics concerning life after death.

As Christians we undoubtedly understand who these entities are and their purpose with interacting with fallen man. Genesis chapter six briefly describes these fallen entities, but the book of Enoch goes into greater detail concerning them. In the Book of Enoch it says that the leader of the fallen angels was called Azazel, and he is often identified with Lucifer 'the Light Bearer' or Lumiel 'the light of God'. He taught men to forge swords and make shields and breastplates.

Azazel also taught them metallurgy and how to mine from the earth and use different metals. To the women he taught the art of making bracelets, ornaments, rings and necklaces from precious metals and stones. He also showed them how to beautify their eyelids and use cosmetic tricks to attract and seduce the opposite sex. From these practices Enoch says there came much Godlessness as humans committed fornication and were led astray becoming corrupt in their ways. The fallen angel Shemyaza, another form of Azazel, is said by Enoch to have taught humans the use of root cuttings and the magical art of enchantment; Shamsiel, the signs of the sun (the solar mysteries); Baraqijal taught astrology; Penemuel instructed humans in the art of writing and reading; Kokabiel, the knowledge of the constellations (astronomy);

Chazaqiel, the knowledge of the clouds and the sky (weather lore and divination); Sariel the courses of the moon (the lunar cycles used in horticulture and agriculture and the esoteric lunar mysteries); and finally Kashdejan taught the diagnosis and healing of diseases and the science of medicine.

Without a doubt there is a great deception taking place in the earth just as Jesus described would take place in the end times, "But as the days of Noah were, so shall also the coming of the Son of man be." We must understand that if we are to travel into the spirit it must be through the door of Jesus Christ otherwise we will be without protection and without fail be utterly deceived by fallen demonic beings.

Make no mistake about it, promoting exploration in the spirit without passing through the blood of Christ is dangerous. Our access point is one of purity by God's method, not the alternative, which is sorcery, witchcraft, and the occult. We pass through the door of Christ rather than climbing in a different way.

2) NIGHT VISIONS

When you begin to go to sleep at night and wake up after your dream, it's a night vision rather than a dream. Here is the distinction: when you're having a dream, you are still in your body; when you're having a night vision, you're traveling in the spirit. After a night vision, you wake up and it's normal to feel a vibration over your being.

Psalm 84:7 says, "They go from strength to strength; each one appears before God in Zion." In the city of God, there are 12 gates, according to the book of Revelation. Not everyone who is taken away in a vision is taken to heaven. There are different realms and places. When you go in the night, God will take you either into those dimensions or perhaps different parts of the earth. In that place, you're in the eternal realm. You gain the ability to move into the future. That's why you've had encounters where you've thought, "Wow, I know I've been here before." That is because in the midst of the night, you've been there in times past.

When you come back from a night vision after waking in the night, take a few moments and pray in the spirit. Let that moment of prayer be an anchor for your memory in that moment. See, most people have dreams or night visions, yet they don't write it down, pray it over, or meditate on it. They fail to anchor it and, as a result, they forget it. Many of you are traveling in the spirit, waking up the next day, and feeling as though you went somewhere in the night. It takes effort, though, to really anchor these things and make the most of them.

The other night, I had an experience in which I was taken into a studio with a friend of mine. The glory was so strong, but I couldn't see my friend's face. I could see he was playing and recording a soaking CD. I came back to myself and that thing started to slip and leave me. I said, "No, no, no, that seed won't be stolen." I began to pray to anchor that memory. I prayed in the spirit and began to focus on what I had seen. The memory came back and that thing began to come back in my room. The next day, I contacted my friend and said, "I saw that you were thinking of making another soaking album" and I began to tell him what I had seen in the night vision. He said, "You don't know how accurate that is. I've been thinking about doing this. This is massive confirmation that I need to do this."

What happened was, I went into the future in the night, saw the vision of what he was supposed to do, and brought it back into the now so that he had the encouragement and grace he needed to start the project. It's a big task and costs a lot of money to record an album like that, especially as a ministry. His natural mind was perhaps at war a bit with what God wanted, and it took a prophetic insight to kickstart the task. God chose a night vision to carry it out.

When you live and move and have your being in Him, you take on His nature. You're in Christ. You gain the ability to be anywhere at anytime. Christ is omnipresent. He is everywhere at once.

The devil hates you because he can't be! In Christ, you now have access to go into places you couldn't in the natural. That is why Paul said, " when you are gathered together, along with my spirit..." (1 Corinthians 5:4, emphasis added).

Was that a mere expression? No. He was accessing this realm as a rightful heir of Christ. Now, that can even happen to your body physically to be in two places at once. You can read of mystics of old who had encounters like this.

I often stay up late at night to pray until the sun comes up the next morning. I was in deep prayer one night and fell into a trance while sitting in my prayer chair. This story has been well-documented so I would like to share it with you. Without going into full detail, in this encounter I met with Kim Jong-un and his sister Kim Yo-jong. This was a secret meeting where I began to speak with them about the denuclearization of their nation. There were several key leaders in this meeting including President Donald Trump.

We discussed peace and I even preached the gospel to him. As I did he began to weep and repent for the past and all that had been done in his nation. We prayed and I knew something had changed. The scene then changed and I saw him step into South Korea. I then found myself back in my home where I was praying, it was a feeling that I had never felt before.

It seemed to me that I was bi-located into the future. That next morning I released a word of what I had experienced the night before. Many people thought I had lost my mind, how could such a thing happen. Kim Jong-un would never step over into South Korea to talk peace. It was unthinkable that he would ever meet with President Donald Trump yet days later the announcement came that something was in the works.

Then a month passed and we saw Kim Jong-un step over into

South Korea. Finally the day came and he met face to face with Donald Trump to discuss the very things that I had seen months prior. In reality, God had bi-located me into the future to be a part of a life changing world event.

VALIDATION AND LEARNING

Some of these things can be hard to swallow for some, under-standably. I was ministering at a church once and sharing on various topics like this and it happened to be at a time of terrible drought. It hadn't rained in over 4 weeks and was consistently about 100 degrees Fahrenheit outside. It was miserably dry. In the midst of my message, I declared, "After my message today, it will pour rain like buckets of water and God will validate what I'm saying to you!"

The service closed and we went out to eat at a restaurant. Not a drop of rain. In the middle of the meal, big black clouds began to form outside. The pastor looked out and dropped his fork. I am eating as quickly as I can because I know heavy rain is coming.

I started to leave and the pastor said, "You can't leave now. This is revival. We need to extend these meetings!" I responded, "This rain is a sign to your people that the rain of God is coming to them." I left and began driving quickly to get out of the area.

The rain started to pour. It came like buckets of water, as I had spoken. It was so intense that I had to pull over in my car. I called Jeff Jansen, quite excited. "Jeff, it hasn't rained here for over 4 weeks. I just prophesied that buckets of water would pour after service. It's pouring so much that I had to pull my car over." He said, "You are stuck in the rain now?" "Yes." He was quick witted, "Next time, prophecy that the rain will come after you leave town."

I say these things not as an anecdote to the message or a mere point of levity, but as a lesson that what God does, He validates. Not only that, but what God does in the spirit must be learned. And finally, all these things are available in Him. He doesn't withhold, rather He gives freely.

There's so much to learn in the kingdom. Even in the natural with doctors, for example, doctors practice medicine. It's not that they've arrived or that they are absolute experts in it all. And guess what: people have no problem going to a doctor that is practicing medicine on them.

However, folks seem to take issue with us practicing the supernatural. Anything we do in God takes practice and involves a learning curve! It should not deter us, but inspire us to go after it. There's plenty of grace in these places for us to learn and stretch.

God is taking the miracle realm and He is bringing it into a convergence with the mystical realm. What does this mean? The miracles, signs, and wonders that we've walked in are meeting the place of seeing in the spirit, and traveling in other realms and dimensions. Why is God doing this? Because there is becoming a problem with mystical-minded folks talking about how they're seeing things, but they aren't manifesting anything. As a result, it creates skepticism in the mind of the hearer.

God is raising up teachers and mystical miracle workers who not only see things in the spirit, but manifest power gifts in the natural. A company of wonder workers are being raised up to teach the body of Christ to access these dimensions — not just to see it, but pull it into the now! This must happen. Your body is your anchor on the earth. Your spirit is in heavenly places. Your soul has the ability to transcend both.

God is moving us to not just perceive with our souls, but bring about the supernatural in our reality here and now. Instead of having mere heavenly visions of a healing Jesus, folks will be manifesting the present healing power of Jesus in sick bodies.

There is such validity in manifestation. That's why Jesus said, "Believe Me that I am in the Father and the Father in Me, or else believe Me for the sake of the works themselves" (John 14:11). In other words, skeptics might not grab hold of your words but they may have more room to grab onto the actual works or miracles. You won't get everyone to believe you. There will always be skeptics toward this brand of spirituality. I've learned to not even answer skeptics.

John Arnott said that one of the biggest mistakes he made in ministry was answering the critics. He said that he should have never answered the critics. They aren't looking for answers; they're looking to pick apart. That's why they always tried to catch Jesus in His words. They didn't want to change. They wanted Christ to change. Their finger pointing didn't have an end goal of learning. It had an end goal of belittling and proving another wrong.

In the next ten years, I believe that these things will become common knowledge. We are simply taking what's in the Word and pulling it out of what's there. We are allowing the God of the Bible to encounter us in the same way we see encounters in His word. For example, theologians will try to theologically explain Isaiah 6 without ever having an Isaiah 6 sort of experience. How can you explain what you haven't experienced? Nevertheless, God is releasing us to experience what we see in the Bible and understand what we see in the Bible.

Let me be emphatically clear, these mystical experiences have to play out practically on the earth. Don't just tell me about slaying giants in the spirit realm. Go feed the poor, clothe the naked, win souls, cast out devils, and care for the hurting. I can have a mystical experience in prayer and it actually empowers me to go out and find broken people on the side of the road and mend their wounds, kiss their face, and give them what they need to get up and bear fruit in the natural. It isn't a mere collection of cloudy experiences in private, but an empowerment to rock the world for Jesus.

3) THE TRANCE REALM

The Hebrew word for the trance realm is mara. This is

perfectly seen where Paul was caught up in the heavens and saw things that he couldn't speak of when he came back down. The difference between the trance realm and the night visions we spoke of earlier is that the trance realm is experienced while awake. The trance realm is a bit of a promotion from night visions because in the trance realm, you are able to access these places while conscious. The reason so many have night visions is because their brain is shut off. Their natural thinking is unplugged and no longer a hindrance for God to take them to spirit places.

The trance realm can be accessed through rest. The Bible describes that we ought to strive to enter into rest. If you're going to strive for anything, strive to rest. Many people strive to see visions and that's why they don't see visions. Strive to rest and all of heaven can begin to download.

 If you're going to strive for anything, strive to rest.

In this place of prayer, you'll begin to feel as though you're asleep. Many teach to rebuke this or dismiss it. Thus, folks jump up and war in tongues to keep themselves awake and out of a slumber-like state. However, they are bypassing the blessing of the trance realm. They are bypassing the process of the natural brain beginning to shut off so that the mind of the spirit can take you. It may feel like falling asleep, but it's not.

The way that I learned this was by me doing my own thing. I

was praying so hard and I got to a place of exhaustion in my early 20's. I said, "Jesus, I can't do this anymore. I can't rebuke anymore. I'm trying, but I'm tired." Then suddenly, I was taken into a trance-like state. I was rebuking what felt like sleep, but actually, I was slipping to a trance. Learn to yield to it, don't fight it.

In this mara realm, the visionary realm starts to come. You begin to experience the invisible becoming visible. The invisible realm is actually more real than the visible realm because it made this realm. Everything in this place is like a hologram. You could put your hand through it or walk through it. It's a spiritual matter. I can see it, but I can't feel it.

4) THE REALM OF APPEARANCE

It isn't until you get to a place called the mareh realm that appearances come. This word is a slightly different Hebrew word than mara in that it invokes an ability to physically touch what is there in a real way. In this place, what we see in the spirit becomes as real as anything in the natural realm. I can reach out and touch what is there. This is what happened to John at Patmos. He was entering a realm of appearance. He felt at Christ's feet as though he was dead. Why? Because he was in the mareh... meaning a dimension that was as real as anything we see in the natural on earth.

I want to say this: when we dive into these places, we aren't trying to control the experience or conjure up a specific happening. When we try to control spiritual experiences, it's called witchcraft. We are simply yielding and allowing God to take us on the journey that He pleases.

When I was 18 years old, I was backslidden. My parents loved the Lord, but I was backslidden and in darkness. When you're a drug addict, you want to experience a greater, purer high, so to speak. I would come to God in prayer with such desire and I'd say, "God, I just want to see You." I would sit before Him and begin to press into these places.

We must trust God, but did you know that God wants to trust us? Certain people couldn't be given spiritual experiences such as this because they couldn't be trusted with it. For example, Paul saw the heavens, but couldn't talk about it. What if God wanted to take you up to have coffee with Moses and a conversation with Paul, but you weren't allowed to say a word? See, some things are too precious for us to speak of. We have to learn the art of having encounters without immediately going out to tell everyone, but instead, waiting for heaven's timing.

A KEY FOR MORE

When I first started seeing signs and wonders in my ministry, I was actually seeing very little. I was so hungry for more. I was sitting with Joshua Mills one day and he gave me a key to unlocking more. He said, "Do you want a key to seeing more miracles, signs, and wonders? Be thankful." It revolutionized my life. I began to thank God for little things that I would see, and suddenly, God would give more. Gratitude became an entryway for increase.

Wonders and signs started to manifest to the tune of gemstones and more showing up in meetings. I will never forget February 28, 2016. It was a life changing moment that taught me much about the realm of thankfulness. As I stood to minister I suddenly went into a trance. The room disappeared, and the heavens opened. I began to peer into heaven where I saw a crystal bowl filled with golden oil. I watched in awe as it began to be poured out like rain. I could see these golden rain drops falling from heaven onto the earth. I shouted to the congregation what I was witnessing. "It's raining in here, golden rain is falling!" The vision finished, and I was back in the meeting and began to thank God for what I was shown.

I asked for the ushers to line people up across the building so that Brynn and I could pray. As we went down the line together the power of God seemed to increase upon touching each individual until we reached one woman in particular. As we placed our hands upon her we could feel the Lightning's of God shoot throughout body. She began to shake violently. The usher was unprepared for such a powerful manifestation and missed catching her and she slammed against the sanctuary floor. As she hit something came flying out of her mouth. I thought to myself, "Did this woman just loose a tooth?"

I walked over to what I believed was a missing tooth only to discover that it was a three-carrot canary diamond in the shape of a raindrop. I picked it up stunned at what I was looking at because it was exactly what I had seen in my vision. I touched it, but it was very soft at first. I said to the Lord, "Why is this so soft?" He said, "Son you are touching something that has just manifested out of the unseen and it has yet to be solidified. Be thankful and gentle with what you are witnessing for it is a holy thing." As I held it in my hand and continued to pray it hardened and began to shine! It was a total manifestation of a sign and wonder that came out of thanksgiving.

Thankfulness became a way for my heart to honor what God was giving. As a result, more began to open up because my heart was being proven before God. The same principles apply to the dimension of seeing! As your heart responds with gratitude for what you see, the Lord begins to pour out more vision, more appearances, and more of Him!

4

A PROPHET'S CREATIVE FUNCTION

"While we do not look at the things which are seen, but at the things which are not seen. For the things which are seen are temporary, but the things which are not seen are eternal."
(2 Corinthians 4:18)

THE BIBLE IS PLAIN THAT THE UNSEEN REALM HAS made everything that we see. The dimensions of the spirit are open to the prophet so that he can begin to see the unseen and, as a result, begin to produce the things that are seen. He uses his words and his mouth to decree and declare the Word of God. It's not a natural language. It's a supernatural language that is inspired by God Himself.

He is able to surpass the three dimensional realm that we live in and come into a place that is beyond 3D and into the realms of God where the spirit realm becomes more real than the chair he sits in or the room he stands in!

There is a higher density or higher dimension available to us. The Bible says, "And we are setting these truths forth in words not taught by human wisdom but taught by the [Holy] Spirit, combining and interpreting spiritual truths with spiritual language [to those who possess the Holy Spirit]" (1 Corinthians 2:13 AMPC).

So, the prophet gives spiritual truths that aren't released with human wisdom, but taught by our guide, the Holy Spirit. He releases spiritual language that has substance, that causes things to be created. There is an interpretation available for this language. It's available only to those full of the Spirit. Spiritual language must be interpreted by the Spirit Himself. When the prophet of God grabs the language of God, he enters what I call a glory portal.

You enter a space in which time is no longer a thing. The future becomes his present moment. He is outside of time and space, dipping into arenas of time that aren't available in the natural. Not only can he see the future, but also the past. It's a literal withdraw on the knowledge of God which exists beyond time. This might sound out there in certain circles, but it shouldn't. This is the normal language and function of God in His people.

The prophet carries the faith of God. What is faith? "Now faith is the substance of things hoped for, the evidence of things not seen" (Hebrews 11:1). Faith is literal substance. The prophet of God carries a literal substance-producing faith that propels words that cause change in our reality. The four dimensions that the prophet of God jumps into, we unpacked in the previous chapter, but I want to explore them in perhaps a new or different light.

CHAZOWN

Chazown, as we discussed earlier, is a divine communication. In the Old Testament, it was translated as vision from the Hebrew language. I want to add, however, that chazown can be described as the audible voice of God. A lot of folks will preach and teach on the inner witness or the inner voice. That's perfectly well, however, chazown is not an inner witness.

This sort of communication is an outer voice. Paul Keith showed me an amazing clip from the life of William Branham. Brother Branham was prophesying from the platform and began declaring a corporate declaration of deliverance over the people there. Demons were being driven out, not just individually, but over the whole crowd. Audibly on the video recording, you can hear the voice of God at the end say, "Amen."

It had me silent for a minute at least. God Himself stepped into the meeting and testified to what the prophet was saying in an audible way, speaking like thunder. Branham says, "Did you hear that? Did you hear that? That is the Lord! He is declaring from heaven that what I am saying to you is the Word of God!"

You could hear His voice rumble through the crowd. Everyone there heard it. This was a display of chazown. It was an audible display of the voice of God. The Lord was proving the authenticity of what the man of God was sharing and prophesying.

As I discussed this with Paul Keith, I felt as though God would begin to show forth these things again. God will bring out things that have taken place in the secret place and make them public and audible. Not only will these things happen, but we'll be able to decipher between the authentic and the pathetic. The prophet is there not just to prophecy, but to establish the very message of the gospel.

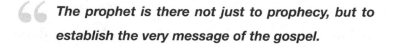

The prophet is there not just to prophecy, but to establish the very message of the gospel.

God is going to begin to manifest signs and wonders that have never been seen before. He also is going to bring back manifestations that haven't been seen for many generations. God Himself will testify to the Word being preached by those walking in true sonship. As a result, the church will know who is walking in true dimensions of the spirit and those who are merely talking.

———

CHEVEZ

Chevez is actually an Aramaic word which means night vision. As you know, it's more than a subconscious experi ence in the night. It's a literal transportation. Upon returning from the night vision, you have the sense that it was a place of travel, not a stationary one. Did you know that these moments can be actual moments of impartation?

There I was eighteen years, old a freshly born-again believer, sitting in my friend's house talking about revival when all of the sudden, a girl to the right of me started weeping and shaking under the power of God. A wind began to blow through that little house and I found myself lying on the floor because of the sheer weight of His presence. Then at that moment I was taken into an open vision.

There I was in the Holy of Holies. The ark of God with the presence of God burning between the cherubs was right in front of me. Out from the midst of the fire came a man dressed in full armor riding on a white horse. The man's eyes where burning like hot coals. A holy fear gripped me as he stopped for a moment to stare into my eyes.

He lifted his sword and pointed it straight at me. Then, without a word spoken between us he began to charge full speed toward me riding upon the white warhorse. I stood there not moving, still in shock from what I was seeing. Just when I thought I would be trampled, the white horse and the burning man who sat upon it entered into me.

Seconds later I found myself back in the room with my friends. By that time, they were laying all over the room weeping, laughing, inebriated under the power of the Holy Spirit.

A heavy cloud of God's presence seemed to rest in that room. I knew from that day on I would never be the same again. The burning man and the white warhorse that I came in contact with was an encounter that I will never forget. It was that day that I recognized that God was looking for fierce warriors for the army of the Lord. I had come in contact with the burning Christ and in turn I became a burning man. My goal in prayer from that day forward has never been to hand God a list of needs, but rather to experience the supernatural dimensions of His spirit!

Kenneth E. Hagin used to have these encounters in the night where his spirit was taken up and he would encounter Christ at night. What was the fruit of these encounters? The man went on to teach generations and nations how to operate in faith on every level of life and his life's impact is still being felt today. Encounters produce fruit. Night visions aren't merely for coffee table talk, but for fruit to show up as a result.

See, these things happen by and with your spirit. Your spirit is the real you. Your body will grow old and fade, but your spirit is renewed and is eternally young. When God gives you a chavez encounter, it's taking place with your spirit.

MARAH

The trance realm can come over you in mystical prayer. As a quick review, don't be afraid to fall into a trance even when it feels like falling asleep. Christian mystics like St. Patrick, for example, understood the trance dimension as being a place of coming into union with God. Paul didn't know if it was in the body or out of the body, he just knew it took place.

There is nothing solid in this realm. It's quite mystical, cloudy, and holographic. It's a territory that many prophets operate in. It has become normal to many. John G. Lake, William Branham, and other forefathers have come into this place. You might think, we've already discussed this. What does this have to do with the prophet's function? Indeed, it has everything to do with the prophet's creative function, for it's in these realms that the spokesperson of God obtains the world-changing Word.

MAREH

Divine appearances are found within this realm. If you can imagine, there is a density available to those who enter this place that is far more real than the other places. When a prophet operates out of this place, the spirit realm is every bit as real as the earth. This is actually the realm in which Paul couldn't tell if he was in the body or out of the body.

This is what Kenneth Hagin and many other scholars would call an "epiphany." T.L. Osborn had an encounter in this realm. Jesus appeared to him and said, "I am the same yesterday, today, and forever." What was the result? God raised up a world-changing evangelist that won souls and brought hope to the masses. The effect that a mareh moment has on a person is lasting and permanent.

The tangible fruit that comes from appearances is profound. It isn't a flimsy happening, but an authentic visitation that causes the person who had it to change the world.

Look at Kenneth Hagin's life, as we've mentioned. Over the course of decades of ministry, he had about 5 appearances of Jesus in what we'd call the mareh realm. What happened as a result was monumental. Jesus gave him messages that he shared with the body of Christ that literally changed the church forever. His teachings have been mass produced, churches have been planted, and his Bible school is running strong today in dozens of nations all over the planet.

I want to be very clear, the appearances he had of Jesus imparted something to him that stuck around. If we are walking in other realms, we will have awesome experiences, which is great! However, when you start experiencing mareh appearances, it will be proven through incredible fruit.

GIFTING VS. CHARACTER

My heart is to see God raise up people who not only see wild things in the spirit and manifest them in the natural, but to see a company of people who have the character it takes to steward such experiences. If a gifting is manifested without underlying integrity, the gifting will actually cost the person greatly. I've asked the Lord that I and many others might walk in the mantle of William Branham, for example, not only that, but to also walk in a character that can be trusted with such gifting.

As I asked the Lord for this, He said to me, "I am preparing them now." See, the vessels are being prepared. How so? Through fire. God purges us from earthly lusts and desires that we might dwell in heavenly places and remain in places of extremely good character that's able to steward extremely powerful gifting.

Moses understood this principle. The Bible says, "By faith Moses, when he was born, was hidden three months by his parents, because they saw he was a beautiful child; and they were not afraid of the king's command. By faith Moses, when he became of age, refused to be called the son of Pharaoh's daughter, choosing rather to suffer affliction with the people of God than to enjoy the passing pleasures of sin, esteeming the reproach of Christ greater riches than the treasures in Egypt; for he looked to the reward. By faith he forsook Egypt, not fearing the wrath of the king; for he endured as seeing Him who is invisible" (Hebrews 11:23-27).

Moses was a powerful, signs-and-wonders-based prophet. Yet his goal wasn't merely great spiritual rank and authority, but to fixate on the invisible God whom he could see through relationship. Moses no longer feared an Egyptian king, but feared the living God.

A GOVERNMENTAL CALL

Moses had his role with the people of God as a prophet. Likewise, Ezekiel was in the mix of God's people as a sort of prophet-pastor. He was in captivity with the Hebrew people and declared the Word of the Lord faithfully. At that same exact time in history, Daniel also was a prophet in Babylon. They were contemporaries and ministered at the same time in the same place. However, their functions were quite different.

Unlike Ezekiel, Daniel was a governmental prophet. God placed him within the kingly structures of his day. He stood in a place with higher ranking officials as a mouthpiece for the Lord. Ezekiel and Daniel may not have even known they were doing the same thing at the same time in different places.

In our time, God is raising up a dual prophetic office. There will be the mystics like Ezekiel who dwell with the people, prophesying the Word of the Lord to the household of faith, and there will be governmental prophets like Daniel, who will stand in earthly structures as an influencer and a change agent in culture and high places. God is interested in touching every sector of society. His plan leaves nothing out. This hour will be one with Daniels and Ezekiels to collaborate in the prophetic throughout the nations. The secular culture will experience the sacred move of the Spirit. No one and nothing will be left out.

The secular culture will experience the sacred move of the Spirit.

The role of the prophet will no longer be an unfamiliar office. We are entering a time in which these prophets will be key change agents in culture. We desperately need a transparency among leadership in regard to the prophetic and how we are seen. God is bringing a bride's revival that will cause everything else to look like a mirage compared to the next move. We have to be so clear and transparent, because what shows up will be things we haven't ever seen or haven't seen for generations. Why do we need to be clear and transparent? Because if we begin to water down the prophetic and water down our experiences, it will undermine the legitimacy of the move of God.

Don't tell people you've been in the appearance realm when you haven't. Don't add fluff to an encounter or go light on areas God wants you to go strong in. We desperately need transparent prophets who will be open about the Word of the Lord to solidify the massive move of God and revival that the Lord will bring.

A CONTINUAL PURSUIT

The position of a prophet is one of continual pursuit and pressing in. I disagree with ministers who stand up and continually say, "We've got everything. We don't need anymore. We've got the fullness." Well, if you've got the fullness, then manifest the fullness! If you have it all, then demonstrate it all. I think it's dangerous to quit a continual pursuit in the name of already having it all.

There are depths that we haven't penetrated, but will happen through pursuit. Listen, I don't want experiences that are outside of the context of what God speaks in His Word. When you remove the cornerstone of Christ, His kingdom, and the Word of God — the whole house falls. Ministries fall, families fall, and societies fall when pursuits for experience are done so outside of the cornerstone of faith in Jesus. With my whole heart, I believe that God will manifest in our generation what He has never manifested before. It will be done on a greater scale.

I was talking to my brother recently. We had a great conversation on the phone for about an hour. I said to him, "I really believe that we are the greatest generation that God has. God has placed us here in this time because He recognizes that He needed to save the best for last."

I will say this, and it might rock some people: if Paul the Apostle was needed in this hour, then God would have waited until now to release Paul. If Moses was needed right now, then God would have waited until now to commence the ministry of Moses. However, they weren't. We were! We are the ones who have been in waiting to be released in this age in this hour. I believe that you are the best seed that God has. He is planting you in a dark time in human history to bring about light and harvest.

Jesus said, "For as in the days before the flood, they were eating and drinking, marrying and giving in marriage, until the day that Noah entered the ark" (Matthew 24:38). Now, there is nothing distinctly unique about eating, drinking, and marrying. That has been happening forever.

So what was Christ saying? There was something unique about eating, drinking, and marrying in Noah's time. It wasn't a natural eating, drinking, and marrying. It was a supernatural eating, drinking, and marrying. It is a partaking of eating, drinking, and being married to Christ. Enoch experienced this, which was a type, pointing to today. He ate of God. He partook of continual fellowship with Him.

A sign of the end times is a union with Christ that involves these three components. At the same time, you have those who are eating, drinking, and marrying a different spirit. That also took place in Noah's time. This was what was happening in Genesis 6 when angels came down and married women. This is happening today as you see trans-genderism being made mainstream, in which demonic self-mutilation is becoming a cultural norm. The definition of marriage is being construed by ancient spirits that have come to manifest darkness in the midst of the earth, as in the days of Noah. You see that the mainstream news stories of today, which involve such perversion, are actually not particularly new to the earth. Many of these themes and issues existed long before. Yet unlike the prophets of old who lived prior to the cross, we live with the power of the resurrection and the truth of the gospel to dispel lies and disband principalities from their places of ruler-ship.

Truth has become revolutionary. It's so rarely declared. The Word of the Lord is being considered hate-speech in many circles. The function of the prophet is to declare a life-giving message of truth, and yet this message isn't being openly received at times. We aren't called to stop our declaration at the sound of critics, instead we are called to advance it!

We are in a day that requires prophets to function in a bold office of breaking the power of principalities off of the lives of people. As we commit ourselves to eat of, drink of, and marry the person of Jesus, we will be empowered to cause a divorce between the world and the demonic spirits that puppet it.

5

FACE TO FACE

"Behold, I stand at the door and knock. If anyone hears My voice and opens the door, I will come in to him and dine with him, and he with Me." (Revelation 3:20)

ACCORDING TO THEOLOGIANS, THERE ARE TWO classification of appearances of God within the Bible. The first is a theophany, which is an appearance of God in the Old Testament. The second is a Christophany, which by definition is an appearance of Christ. Traditionally, this term references visions of Christ after His ascension. The bright light that Paul experienced would be an example of a Christophany. Within church history, there are those who have not just reached out and touched the Holy Spirit, but have had direct contact with Jesus Christ Himself.

In recent years, there has been a teaching growing up in the church that attempts to dismiss any and all attempts at having a face-to-face encounter with Jesus. The idea is that if you seek after such experiences, you could be deceived. The teaching says that Satan could come as an angel of light and deceive us.

The reality is, you and I are the only beings made in the image of God. In seeking after a face-to-face encounter with Jesus, Satan cannot come and emulate Christ or take on His image to interweave himself into our encounter with God. It's a deception free zone.

It's an old tradition that says we should just wait till we get to heaven before we seek an encounter, face to face, with Jesus. It's not in the Scriptures, however. Jesus said that when we gather in His name, He is here in the midst of us. What does that look like? It certainly isn't a mere figure of speech or sentimental saying. It's a living reality that Christ will break through into our presence with His visual and literal reality!

What was John unpacking when he said, "I will come in to him and dine with him"? He was expressing one thing: fellowship. A church without fellowship is nothing but a warehouse. It's a storage facility. Fellowship will always lead you to partnership. Partnership will always lead you to supernatural supply. Supply will always lead you to a supernatural distribution.

 A church without fellowship is nothing but a warehouse.

When you come into Christ, there will be an undeniable manifestation on your life. People will not only recognize that Christ lives in you, but He is manifesting through your mortal flesh! "He who has My commandments and keeps them, it is he who loves Me. And he who loves Me will be loved by My Father, and I will love him and manifest Myself to him" (John 14:21, emphasis added).

The word manifest here means to appear, to shine, to transfigure, or to illuminate. Jesus wasn't saying, "I will hover over your gatherings which you have once per week and politely bless your three points and a poem."

He was literally declaring Himself as willing and ready to manifest His awesome power and presence in our very midst as we come after Him wherever we are.

The western church has so diluted the authentic gospel. Christ's intention for the church wasn't organized religion full of tradition. It wasn't to hide behind four walls of the church. No. The intention for the church was to build a supernatural organization sent from heaven to manifest the heavenly kingdom on the earth. It was to release the blueprint of heaven onto the earth so the earth looks more like heaven as the church gets more vocal.

Religion draws a line in the sand and says, "If you go over this line, you become a fanatic." Religion carries an attitude that declares, "Brother, you can talk about Jesus, just don't talk about seeing Jesus face to face. That is a little too loopy for us. We have to wait until we die to experience that."

Jesus declared that He is the way, the truth, and the life (see John 14). He did not say that He is the way, the truth, and the death. It isn't only in death that we experience Him. It's here and now in this life that we experience Him! Don't delay your encounter with God for a later-date or for the hereafter. We have no business postponing the move of God!

"Now the Lord is the Spirit; and where the Spirit of the Lord is, there is liberty. But we all, with unveiled face, beholding as in a mirror the glory of the Lord, are being transformed into the same image from glory to glory, just as by the Spirit of the Lord" (2 Corinthians 3:17-18). Don't you see? Beholding the person of Jesus is the process by which we transform! We can literally manifest Jesus to such a degree that people see Jesus when they see us!

Paul said that it's in Him that we live and move and have our being! So when Paul was showing up to town, it was just as if Jesus Himself was showing up in town... casting out devils, preaching the gospel, healing the sick, and raising the dead! This isn't bizarre or off-base Christianity... this is Christianity at its finest! Whole groups of people are writing books about how we as a movement are "strange fire," among other things. No, we are just fresh fire! We have the real thing... an authentic burning passion to see Jesus manifest to us, and through us to a lost and dying world.

When did the body of Christ become a place where the degrees before and after your name determine the authenticity of the gospel that you preach? This isn't the original design! The gospel was fashioned by God to be a message beyond words. It was and is to be a message of the demonstration of power.

BIBLICAL APPEARANCES

I've found 13 times in the gospels and the book of Acts where Jesus manifested Himself in an actual appearance to a person or people. The accounts and Scripture references are detailed below.

1. The first was His appearance to Mary Magdalene. (Mark 16:9-11)
2. After that, He showed Himself to other women at the tomb. (Matthew 28:8-10)
3. Later, He showed Himself to Peter. (Luke 24:32)
4. Then He showed up and shared with two travelers on the road to Emmaus. (Mark 16:12-13)
5. Following that, He appeared to the ten disciples behind closed doors. (Luke 24:36-42)
6. Then later, He showed Himself to all the disciples. This was when He proved Himself to Thomas. (John 20:26-31)
7. Seven disciples saw Jesus later while fishing and they ate food together and fellowshipped. (John 21:1-14)
8. Eleven disciples on the mountain saw Jesus. (Matthew 28:16-20)
9. A crowd of 500 individuals witnessed Christ ascending into heaven. (1 Corinthians 15:7)

10. Jesus' brother James saw Jesus after the transfiguration. (1 Corinthians 15:7)
11. Many saw Christ ascend to heaven after He taught them for 40 days. (Luke 24:44-49)
12. Paul saw Jesus on the road to Damascus. (Acts 9:3-9)
13. Stephen saw Jesus just before being martyred for his ministry. (Acts 7:55-56)

It's a widespread church understanding that Thomas is called "doubting Thomas." Not such an endearing term. Why did he want to touch Christ to believe? Because Thomas wanted to verify the reality of this thing, considering he was putting his whole life on the line by following Jesus. A commitment to Christianity in that day was a death sentence. He wanted to get ahold of a living vision and appearance of Jesus. In a sense, I can't blame him. If my life is being put on the line for a message, I want to encounter that message tangibly.

AN ELIJAH-LIKE CHALLENGE

There is a place in India called Kerala. I've been there. Thomas actually went there and observed the Brahmin priests. They would worship the sun and throw water up in the air and it would fall back down. Thomas observed this for three days. So he walked down to the priests after three days and said, "Why doesn't your god receive your sacrifice?" They said, "What do you mean?" He said, "You throw the water up to your sun god as a sacrifice, but he doesn't receive it. It just falls back down to you."

With that, Thomas presented an Elijah-like challenge. He said, "I'm going to pray to my God, and when I do, I will throw water up in the air and it will remain suspended in the air." Of course, they were totally skeptical. So Thomas said, "Lord, I've seen You face to face. Thank You for signs and wonders."

Thomas threw the water into the air and the water remained suspended in mid air for three days. Every single one of the Brahmin priests got born again and followed the way of Christianity. The whole area was swept into the gospel and to this day, it is the most Christian region in all of India. Thomas needed a tangible experience. That tangible experience anchored him to a world-changing message. That world changing message has impacted the regions he worked in... not just for a moment, but for the generations that came after him! Oh if Thomas could only see the lasting impact of his work in Kerala.

YESTERDAY, TODAY, AND FOREVER

T.L. Osborn was a missionary in India. In fact, he was a failed missionary. He would go and bring the scriptures with nothing else. The locals wouldn't receive his words. Burnt out and discouraged, he moved back to America. After coming to the States to pastor a small church, he was down-trodden and depressed, on the brink of quitting the ministry all together. In the summer of 1949 in Portland, Oregon, T.L.'s wife, Daisy, went to a William Branham meeting.

After listening and observing, she went home and told T.L. that he needed to come to the meeting. He was reluctant, but finally yielded. In the meeting, William Branham brought a young man on stage who was deaf and mute. In front of the whole crowd, the boy's ears were opened and his tongue completely loosed by the power of God.

T.L said, "I heard within myself the sound of a thousand voices, as if from eternity's past, and they said, 'you can do that!'"

He went home and locked himself in his bedroom for three days. He didn't eat or drink water. He said, "I will not leave my room unless I have a face-to-face encounter with Jesus." After three days, Jesus walked through the wall and met with T.L. He looked at him directly and said very simply, "I am the same yesterday, today, and forever." He turned and walked out of the room. T.L. was so radically transformed by the experience that he immediately went to Jamaica and set up crusades.

What was supposed to be a three day meeting ended up lasting six weeks. Eighty-nine deaf mutes in his first campaign were completely healed. Just one encounter with the Lord Jesus will change everything.

George and Stephen Jeffries are another prime example of a radical abandonment toward God. They were preachers from Wales who began Elim church. They would gather at church without an itinerary or schedules. There was no sermon or worship planned. They would simply pray and seek to see Jesus Himself. Finally, one day while praying, Jesus manifested Himself on the wall of that church. For three solid hours, they beheld Him. Strangers that weren't even a part of the church would come off of the street and be drawn in by God's presence. They described what they knew to be the crucified Lamb who was slain. The impact was immeasurable.

George and Stephen had a specific anointing to see crippled and arthritic joints and limbs restored. It has been said that sitting in their meetings was noisy. It would sound like shot guns going off as limbs would straighten up and joints would realign and pop back into place. They walked in a powerful anointing to see such things healed. One particular man had a leg that was about 6 inches shorter than the other. He came in on a crutch. Stephen prayed for him on stage in front of everyone. His leg grew out in front of the entire congregation, completely healed and restored. The man jumped up and sprinted around the platform completely free! You don't know what will open up to you when you simply seek after a face-to-face meeting with Jesus.

St. Francis of Assisi encountered Jesus in 1224. As a result, he began to bear the marks Christ on his physical body. Not only that, but miracles and demonstrations of power began to manifest wherever he would go. Julian of Norwich is another mystic and theologian of old who met Jesus. She was on her death bed at a young age. Jesus came to her seven different times. She was completely healed and became the first woman to ever write a book in English.

The book was called Revelations of Divine Love. It's still available, in fact. As a family, we went into Julian of Norwich's prayer room in England. When we walked in, my daughter (who was already hyped up on chocolate) stopped and said, "I want to pray." So we all began praying. The presence of God was so made manifest in that room that even our kids were engaged with what was happening in the spirit in that place.

Sailing back to America from England, John Wesley told the Lord, "I will read the book of Ephesians one hundred times." On the one hundredth read, Wesley looked up and saw Jesus staring at him. This encounter sparked the Great Awakening, and when he got back to the States, the power of God manifested and the nation was rocked in an irreversible way. History tells us that when Wesley spoke in these meetings, it was like people were mowed down by the power of God.

An encounter with Jesus, like these mighty people of faith had, will produce such unique power on our lives and ministries. It will bear fruit and produce results that can't be mimicked. One of my fathers in the faith said to me, "They can copy your sermons. They can steal your notes. But they can't duplicate the supernatural power."

When you have an encounter with God, people can steal your messages, your words, or your quotes, but they cannot duplicate the power of God. There is no faking the real supernatural power of God. There is no fabricating it when you've spent time with Jesus. Your audience can sniff out what is legitimate and what is not. Authenticity is a commodity that the world is truly craving! We must give it.

I know of a great prophet of old who was spending time with Jesus, desiring to walk in sign and wonders desperately. He prayed, paced, rocked, and sought. For extended periods of time, he would simply cry out to God to move in the power of God. Finally, one day, he was taken up in a vision with Jesus to the throne of the Father. He heard the Father say to him, "Son, what do you want?" He cried out with the loudest voice possible, "I want to move in signs and wonders!" The Lord responded, "Son, what do you want?" Not understanding why he wasn't being heard by God, he cried out again, "I want to move in signs and wonders!" God responded still with the same tone and question, "Son, what do you want?" Finally, he cried out with the same loud and passionate voice, "God! I want You!"

When he declared that, God began to laugh. Not just laugh, but belly laugh! In that moment, something like a brand came from the throne and hit him in his chest. In that moment, he fell back into his own body. What a powerful declaration!

The glory of God was surging through him and he knew that he had seen God face to face and would never be the same.

He knew that signs and wonders would from then on follow his ministry.

Sure enough, he went to his very next week and miracles began happening to the tune of missing limbs growing back. Outbreaks of signs and wonders started to become normal in his meetings. Why? Because in the secret place, he didn't merely pursue miracles and desire the power of God, but he desired God Himself. In all of our pursuits, may God Himself be the one we crave. The encounters we are brought into from that place will catapult us into depths and realms that we didn't formerly know existed.

PURSUIT

A Divine Catching-Up...

THE BIBLE DESCRIBES HOW CERTAIN PEOPLE WALKED with God. For example, Enoch walked with God for 365 years and then was suddenly taken. The word walk in the Hebrew is the word halak. This word in the Hebrew is quite interesting and means more than to walk with your legs forward or backward. It connotes to go up and down, in and out, and to and fro in God. There is a realm that we can walk (or halak) in which we can't tell whether we are on the earth or in heavenly places. Christians aren't called to live outside of God's presence and outside of these realms, but rather in them!

God's presence is the central matter when it comes to walking with God. The presence of God is far more than a feeling. I'm amazed at how people can grow tired of feeling

God's presence. Consider it with me: people in heaven have been there for eons of time and have felt God's presence from the moment they arrived, but they aren't tired of it. Why? Because the presence is not a feeling, it's a Person who brings a revelation that you can feast on. When you begin to live out of a revelation of the presence of God, it never grows tiresome.

People ask me, "What is your favorite place that you ever travel to?" I tell them, "My favorite place to be is the presence of God." It doesn't matter what nation or location I find myself in, it's the presence of God that I enjoy above all. It's the location outside of time, beyond corruption and decay, where sweet fellowship takes place. This is the place we live in and feast from.

Do you remember what Christ said to Satan while on the backside of the desert? The temptation was on and Jesus rebuked Satan with these words: "It is written, 'Man shall not live by bread alone, but by every word that proceeds from the mouth of God'" (Matthew 4:4). Notice, He said "every word that proceeds." In other words, there is a continual procession coming from the mouth of God. It's an ongoing leading of progressive revelation... a never ending journey into an ever increasing glory. Because of this, when we think that we have God figured out, He will do a new thing, reveal a new side of Himself, and present truth in a new way. He isn't stale or outdated. He also isn't so small that we can pin Him under a microscope and "figure Him out." He is vast, eternal, and ever revealing. In this, God renews the responsibility in us to draw us deeper in Him.

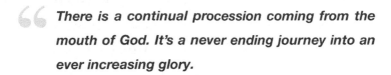

> **There is a continual procession coming from the mouth of God. It's a never ending journey into an ever increasing glory.**

Jeremiah said, "For who has stood in the counsel of the Lord, and has perceived and heard His word?" (Jeremiah 23:18). The word stood means to constantly stand steadfast and abide in the presence. Some people live in seasons in the presence and somehow they fall out of step. As a result, God will call us and then cause us to renew the revolution that He called us to walk into in the first place. Standing before God is not seasonal, but permanent.

Adam, for example, walked with God in the cool of the day consistently. In fact, after breaking down the original text, the Bible says that the Word of God came walking to Adam in the cool of the day. Did you know that the Word of God has legs? Yes, revelation has legs! God's plan to reveal Himself and His truth is mobile and able to meet us. Jesus is the ultimate example of a walking revelation. Look at Christ on the road to Emmaus, for example: He was giving revelation to the disciples on the road, yet they didn't perceive Him. Why? Because He came in a new form.

See, many Christians experience similar murkiness when encountering God. They met Jesus in one fashion and, as a result, they don't realize He will change it up and take on a new form as the relationship continues. He will appear in new ways and speak new things. Continually learn Him.

It isn't about what proceeded, past tense, from the mouth of God. It's about what is proceeding, present tense. What is proceeding is what positions us to actually receive His outpouring.

People live in capsules of time and never move forward after encountering God. In other words, they have a powerful moment with God. Then, instead of seeking new ones and pursuing progressive understanding, they just sit in that moment of time — as though they have God pegged in that place. As a result, they are no longer conquerors of time, but victims of time. Because they're victims of time, they simply live in nostalgia, wishing they could go back to when God was working in their lives instead of moving ahead and experiencing the newness.

FOOD OF THE SUPERNATURAL VARIETY

I read a book in Bible college called *Lilies Amongst Thorns* by Danyun. In the book, Brother Yun was highlighted. He is an exiled Chinese evangelist and gospel preacher. Brother Yun had been imprisoned for 81 days because of his Christian faith. They found a Bible on him and threw him in a dungeon as a result.

They would come into the dungeon and beat him daily and refused to feed him. For the first 15 days, he had no food or water. On that fifteenth day, as he was worshipping God in the dungeon, Jesus walked through the wall and brought bread and wine to him. For the next seventy-plus days, Jesus would walk into his cell every single day and give him bread and wine.

There is a mystery and even mystical reality in Christianity that is being released in this hour. There are revelations and realms that the church has long forgotten about. God wants to re-reveal those paths so that we can begin to walk in this presently. Intimacy in the presence of Jesus will cause you to forge new paths and become a pioneer of the unseen. Substance is created through intimacy.

Manifestations in a person's ministry don't happen because someone spent years in the seminary. It happens only through intimacy with Jesus Christ. Looking at Him face to face in whatever forms He comes in will brand you in an irreversible way. It's a contagious atmosphere. This is the key to manifestations of power, not mere Bible knowledge and degrees. A personal exchange with God causes us to be enabled to dispense His great grace in the places He calls us.

When Paul wrote Colossians, he used the word mustérion, which is where we get our word mystery or mystic. He told them, "To them God willed to make known what are the riches of the glory of this mystery among the Gentiles: which is Christ in you, the hope of glory" (Colossians 1:27, emphasis added). In other words, Jesus Christ is the mystery of heaven.

He was the sacred secret, a mystical Christ who *has been* revealed. Yet not only revealed, but is ever being revealed! As we approach Him, an addiction for Him enters our heart. See, Paul talked about his desire for Christ to be formed in the people of God. As we are continually attentive to the new forms Christ takes in our lives, He is thereby continually formed in our being. Seeing His form, forms Him in us.

THE ENCOUNTERS OF THE SAINTS

Most people never read the book of Job, particularly people who are heavily grace-oriented. They feel that it's a book of sorrows and brokenness and not new-creation sort of matter. However, Job has some of the deepest mysteries of the unseen realm and was written before the law.

Thus, Job's revelation was not based on principles or tablets of stone, but a relationship. The Bible speaks of Job remembering the days in which God was above him like a flame of fire and his steps were bathed with oil (see Job 29:6). Job walked with the Lord in such a way that he moved in and with God's presence.

Even as Job would slip into God's presence, so we also have the same opportunity. Have you ever been in a conversation with someone and suddenly you slip out of it and God takes you somewhere else with your gaze and focus? Some people say that the Holy Spirit is a gentleman, and I believe that. However, the Holy Spirit will sometimes rip you out of the moment you're in and take you into new places in the spirit.

The fourth and fifth century church fathers understood something about this.

They were called "the desert fathers." They would go into the desert, escaping the natural world, to experience the presence of God. They so longed for God to come upon them that they shunned earthly things to position themselves with only one person to lean on, Jesus. They would be caught up in ecstatic revelations. Christ would appear to them.

There was a catholic saint named St. Teresa of Avila who would spend hours and hours with Jesus. So much so that when she was worshipping the Lord, an angel came in with a spear and pierced her heart. She said, "It was as though fire burned in my heart and I couldn't live one day without Him." When St. Teresa died and went to be with Jesus in eternity, they took her actual heart out of her body and there was a literal, physical piercing on the flesh of her heart. They said they didn't even know how she lived. Intimate times with the Holy Spirit will cause you to realize that the reality of the unseen realm is more real than the chair you're sitting on.

Catherine of Siena was another old time saint of God. She said that the Lord walked in and took her heart out of her body, and for three solid months, she walked around saying, "I don't have a heart anymore because the Lord stole my heart." After three months, the Lord walked back into her room while she was worshipping and put His heart in her chest. The reality of heaven is so real, it will brand you in the physical.

As we live in Jesus, we breathe the rarified air of heaven. We take in His eternal presence. Our very atmosphere is that of heaven. Thus, we are sustained. We aren't continuing to tick merely because of natural food and earthly things, but we are nourished through the literal sustenance of His person. This is why Brother Yun could go 81 days without eating or drinking in the natural... because Jesus gave him something beyond it. He was so enraptured by Jesus in those days that by the eighty-first day when they came in to beat him, they no longer saw Brother Yun, but they saw the face of Jesus on him. How? Because you start to look like who you spend time with.

The body of Christ is not the building you gather in. I love church settings, church buildings, and church gatherings. We shouldn't forsake it. However, the body of Jesus is the spiritual and physical body that we can enter into. Christ on the throne is seated there in a glorified body. God is a Spirit, yes, but He also dwells in a body. Christ took on human flesh and didn't take it off, but instead was glorified in it and is now seated in a body on the throne. He wanted to wear humanity. Christ is the new and living way. His flesh was torn, which was the veil of human flesh separating us from divinity. His body was broken to clear the way and remove the barricade between people and their Creator.

"In disquieting thoughts from the visions of the night, when deep sleep falls on men, fear came upon me, and trembling, which made all my bones shake. Then a spirit passed before my face; the hair on my body stood up. It stood still, but I could not discern its appearance. A form was before my eyes; there was silence; then I heard a voice..." (Job 4:13-16).

Job, spending time with God, entered a place of seeing in the spirit. Visions began to flow. Job was awakened in the spirit realm to something new happening... so much so, that his physical body responded by his hair standing up, his body trembling, and his bones shaking! Notice, Job didn't see anything at first. He didn't see a clear image of the form of the Holy Spirit. Rather, it was a mystical experience that lead to revelation. It's a mistake to think that an instant clarity will always be given when coming across the things of the Spirit. The biblical model for encountering mystical things is quite clear: additional revelation is often needed to decipher that which was shown. Many enigmas exist in the spirit, however, the Holy Spirit is our guide to solve the riddles and make clear what was once murky.

Standing before God gives you access to these Job 4 sort of experiences. Not only that, but these experiences boost you into a place in which you're able to bring the wild revelations from the spirit into the natural to see about change. There is a weighty Word in the spirit realm for you to access, and when you do, you'll be able to bring it into the natural world to change history and break the main-frame of society, so to speak. Nothing will be left the same!

You can always tell the substance of a man's life and his relationship with God by the physical manifestations that they have. Manifestations reveal the glory on someone. It's not just having a good story about going to heaven, it's the weight upon the words that they're speaking that reveal to you whether or not they've been there. Manifestation reveals the reality of the place that you've been. When you're walking with heaven in heavenly places, the reality of heaven begins to be manifested so much so that irrational and illogical things that could never happen start to happen. Why? Because you are using the actual substance of God's presence to bring about His reality into our reality.

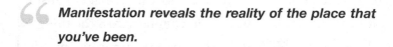

> **Manifestation reveals the reality of the place that you've been.**

The more time you spend with God, the more the density of His presence begins to be realized. Density is what gives something weight. Something heavy is dense with particles. It's packed full of matter in a tight space, making it heavy. In God, His glory becomes more and more dense in our lives the more time we spend with Him. He packs power into our beings, our lives, and our ministries as we open our hearts to His total infilling.

We cannot afford to miss this life. It's not an aspect of life. It is life itself. There is a divine catching up that takes place. Jesus will come to you like fire, like honey, like wine, or perhaps something else. He will manifest according to the need of the moment. You might think, I don't have time for this sort of life. Look, the scripture says that Enoch walked with God for 65 years and then lived for another 300 years — walking with God the whole time. Why does that matter? Because even though Enoch had domestic responsibilities and perhaps a full schedule with family, employment, and so forth, it didn't keep him from pursuing a deep place in God.

Don't think that your schedule is too full for God. Don't think that the busyness of life is a sufficient excuse to keep you from walking with God as Enoch did. You are able to make time for the things you value. It's crucial that we begin to value a deep intimacy with God above the cares of this life. In such a perspective, making time for Him will come as natural as breathing.

In making time for God and drinking of His presence, open yourself to the new form He is taking on in your life. Let yourself slip into the spirit. Let yourself experience in the physical what God is manifesting from the heavenly place.

It's the life you were born for.

7

CLOSING THOUGHTS

An Ancient Path that's Waiting for Us

IF CHRIST IS BOTH THE WAY AND THE DOOR INTO Heaven, how can we find this path of mystery; this door into the unseen? Jesus Christ; the mystic staircase and vehicle of supernatural power, the very throne of grace and mercy resting over the Ark of the Covenant, hidden from ages, is waiting to be discovered. When we turn our full attention upon the beauty of Christ we will discover the ancient path that leads us to everlasting life.

Leonard Ravenhill has often been quoted as saying, "No man is greater than his prayer life." And while we recognize that prayer is a vital part of every Christian's walk with God, the kind of prayer that's offered is necessary to see into the *unseen*. There seems to be those throughout history who encountered heaven in a much deeper way.

Those whom Isaiah spoke of; who fly like cloud, like doves to their windows. Let what you've gathered in the former pages embark you on this journey into the unseen realms of mystical prayer and hidden secrets in the Holy Spirit.

Let yourself walk with God in a much deeper and intimate way than you ever knew was possible. You will discover a prayer life that erases all barriers between you and God. You'll enter a realm where deep calls out to the deep and revelation flows freely from the throne of Grace.

The action that follows instruction is far more important than simply reading the instruction. Let action follow this reading. Let the inspiration of the saints of old push you to a greater depth of *experience*.

For so long, the body of Christ has kept the Lord at arms-length. We have wanted Him to be around us, but the thought of Him flooding us seems a bit too intimidating. We have wanted the thought of God in our lives but not the reality of God in our lives.

We've wanted the conveniences of Christian faith without the conviction and call of Christian faith. I pray that such thinking would be dispelled from your mental faculties permanently. May we dive into the very life that Jesus died for us to experience.

The world is waiting for you to show up with something more than mere words and mere theology. As good as sound theology is, it won't manifest the glory of God. Only true *intimacy* and *mystical prayer* will do that.

CHAPTER ONE DISCUSSION

Contemplation Prayer

1) HOW CAN CONTEMPLATION PRAYER CHANGE THE WAY
YOU COMMUNE WITH GOD?

_____

_____

_____

_____

_____

_____

2) HAVE YOU EXPERIENCED GOD IN PRAYER? HOW DID IT
EFFECT YOU?

_____

_____

_____

_____

_____

_____

3) WHICH STAGES OF CONTEMPLATION HAVE YOU EXPERI-
ENCED? WHICH STAGE ARE YOU MOST INTERESTED IN
EXPLORING AND WHY?

_____

_____

_____

_____

_____

_____

MYSTICAL CHALLENGE:

TAKE TIME IN PRAYER THIS WEEK TO INTENTIONALLY
EXPLORE CONTEMPLATION PRAYER. FIND YOURSELF
MOVING INTO EACH OF THE 4 STAGES OF THIS PLACE
IN GOD.

RECORD YOUR EXPERIENCES BELOW:

_____

_____

_____

_____

_____

_____

_____

_____

_____

CHAPTER ONE DECREE:

> *I DECREE AND DECLARE THAT MY PRAYER LIFE WILL NEVER BE THE SAME. I SHALL STEP INTO NEW PLACES OF CONTEMPLATION AND DEPTH. DISTRACTIONS WILL DISSOLVE, CARES AND CONCERNS WILL FALL OFF, AND MY WHOLE SPIRIT, SOUL, AND BODY WILL REMAIN FIXED ON THE PERSON OF JESUS. THE STAGES OF CONTEMPLATION PRAYER ARE MINE TO EXPLORE, IN JESUS NAME!*

CHAPTER TWO DISCUSSION

The Prayer of the Mystic

1) PRACTICALLY SPEAKING, HOW CAN YOU GROW IN YOUR FRIENDSHIP WITH HOLY SPIRIT?

_____

_____

_____

_____

_____

_____

2) THE CHAPTER MENTIONS THE DANGERS OF COMPARISON. HOW DOES COMPARING YOUR ENCOUNTER WITH SOMEONE ELSE'S ENCOUNTER HINDER PRAYER?

_____

_____

_____

_____

_____

_____

3) WHAT PRECONCEIVED NOTIONS TOWARD PRAYER HAVE
YOU HAD TO SHAKE OFF IN ORDER TO EXPERIENCE GOD'S
FULLNESS?

_____

_____

_____

_____

_____

MYSTICAL CHALLENGE:

THIS WEEK, PLACE SPECIAL FOCUS ON YOUR FRIENDSHIP
WITH HOLY SPIRIT. BE ATTENTIVE TO THE FRUIT OF THIS
PURSUIT.

RECORD YOUR EXPERIENCES BELOW:

_____

_____

_____

_____

_____

_____

_____

_____

CHAPTER TWO DECREE:

66 *I DECREE AND DECLARE THAT MY FRIENDSHIP WITH HOLY SPIRIT SHALL BE AS FLUID AND SIMPLE AS BREATHING. I RENOUNCE ANY FRIENDSHIP WITH DARKNESS AND COVENANTS I'VE MADE WITH FALSE IDEAS. THIS DAY AND EVERYDAY, I CHOOSE PARTNERSHIP WITH THE PRECIOUS HOLY SPIRIT, MY COMFORTER, GUIDE, AND FRIEND, IN JESUS NAME!*

CHAPTER THREE DISCUSSION

The Four Dimensions of Seeing

1) DOES YOUR PRAYER LIFE FEEL ONE DIMENSIONAL? HOW CAN YOU ENTER NEW DIMENSIONS WITH EASE?

_____

_____

_____

_____

_____

_____

2) WHAT IMPACT SHOULD THE REALMS OF SEEING HAVE ON A BELIEVER'S LIFE?

_____

_____

_____

_____

_____

_____

3) THE CHAPTER MENTIONS THE VALUE OF GRATITUDE. HOW HAVE YOU SEEN GRATITUDE POSITIVELY EFFECT YOUR FAITH WALK?

_____

_____

_____

_____

_____

_____

MYSTICAL CHALLENGE:

ASK THE LORD TO TAKE YOU INTO THE REALMS OF SEEING FROM THIS CHAPTER. LET GOD CHALLENGE OLD, ANTI-QUATED IDEAS ABOUT WHAT PRAYER IS OR ISN'T. FULLY OPEN YOURSELF TO THE POSSIBILITIES CONTAINED IN THESE REALMS.

RECORD YOUR EXPERIENCES BELOW:

_____

_____

_____

_____

_____

_____

_____

_____

_____

CHAPTER THREE DECREE:

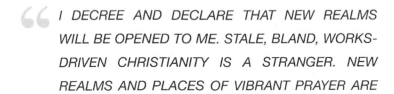 *I DECREE AND DECLARE THAT NEW REALMS WILL BE OPENED TO ME. STALE, BLAND, WORKS-DRIVEN CHRISTIANITY IS A STRANGER. NEW REALMS AND PLACES OF VIBRANT PRAYER ARE MY NEW NORM, IN JESUS NAME!*

CHAPTER THREE DECADE.

CHAPTER FOUR DISCUSSION

A Prophet's Creative Function

1) BASED ON THE TEACHING, HOW WOULD YOU DESCRIBE A MODERN PROPHET TO SOMEONE WHO ASKED?

_____

_____

_____

_____

_____

_____

2) WHAT IS THE RESULT OF WALKING IN GIFTING WITHOUT GODLY CHARACTER?

_____

_____

_____

_____

_____

_____

3) PROPHETS (AND ALL CHRISTIANS) MUST DECLARE WHAT GOD IS SAYING. HAVE YOU FOUND THAT TO BE CHALLENGING AT TIMES? HOW DID YOU OVERCOME THAT?

_____

_____

_____

_____

_____

_____

MYSTICAL CHALLENGE:

THIS WEEK, PROPHESY WHAT GOD IS SAYING OVER YOUR LIFE AND THE WORLD AROUND YOU. TAKE TIME TO HEAR FROM THE HEART OF GOD CONCERNING THAT WHICH CONCERNS YOU. ALSO, AS YOU READ THE *WRITTEN* WORD, LET IT BE TO YOU A *SPOKEN* WORD FROM HEAVEN.

RECORD THE PROPHECIES BELOW:

_____

_____

_____

_____

_____

_____

_____

_____

_____

CHAPTER FOUR DECREE:

 I DECREE AND DECLARE THAT PROPHETIC UTTERANCE SHALL FLOW FROM MY BELLY LIKE A RIVER. MY EYES ARE OPEN, MY EARS ARE UNBLOCKED, AND THE PROPHETIC GRACE OF THE HOLY GHOST IS UPON ME. I WILL HEAR WHAT COMES FROM THE LIPS OF GOD AND BECOME THE LIPS OF GOD IN MY HOME, MY COMMUNITY, MY WORKPLACE, AND MY GENERATION, IN JESUS NAME!

CHAPTER FIVE DISCUSSION

Face to Face

1) HOW HAVE PEOPLE NOTICED CHRIST'S MANIFESTATION IN YOUR LIFE?

_____

_____

_____

_____

_____

_____

2) IF JESUS APPEARED TO YOU TODAY, WHAT WOULD HE SAY? HOW MIGHT HE ENCOURAGE YOU?

_____

_____

_____

_____

_____

_____

3) BASED ON THE STORIES IN THE CHAPTER, WHAT CHAR-
ACTERISTICS FOLLOW THOSE WHO HAVE HAD FACE TO
FACE ENCOUNTERS WITH GOD?

_____

_____

_____

_____

_____

_____

MYSTICAL CHALLENGE:

THIS WEEK, ASK THE LORD FOR FACE TO FACE EXPERI-
ENCE WITH HIM. BELIEVE FOR GOD TO TAKE YOU TO NEW
PLACES OF INTIMACY IN HIM. STUDY THE FACE TO FACE
ENCOUNTERS OF THE SAINTS OF OLD AND LET THE FATHER
DUPLICATE THEM IN YOUR MIDST.

RECORD YOUR EXPERIENCES BELOW:

_____

_____

_____

_____

_____

_____

_____

_____

_____

CHAPTER FIVE DECREE:

 I DECREE AND DECLARE THAT I WILL NOT BE A PRODUCT OF RELIGION. I AM A PRODUCT OF GRACE. AS A RESULT, FACE TO FACE ENCOUNTERS WITH THE LORD SHALL BE MY REALITY. I AM MOVING INTO A PLACE OF VISITATION, APPEARANCES, VISIONS, DREAMS AND ENCOUNTERS, IN JESUS NAME!

CHAPTER SIX DISCUSSION

Pursuit

1) WHAT DO YOU IMAGINE ENOCH'S WALK WITH GOD LOOKED LIKE? HOW CAN YOU DUPLICATE IT?

_____

_____

_____

_____

_____

_____

2) JOB'S STEPS WERE BATHED IN OIL. WHAT DOES THIS MEAN AND HOW CAN YOU EXPERIENCE THE SAME THING?

_____

_____

_____

_____

_____

_____

3) THE CHAPTER SAYS THAT JESUS WILL MANIFEST HIMSELF ACCORDING TO THE NEED IN THE MOMENT. WHAT DO YOU NEED RIGHT NOW?

_____

_____

_____

_____

_____

_____

MYSTICAL CHALLENGE:

THIS WEEK, LET YOUR PURSUIT INCREASE. BE WATCHFUL OF THE VARIETY OF WAYS JESUS MANIFESTS HIMSELF ACCORDING TO THE NEED OF THE MOMENT. TAKE NOTE OF THE WAYS THAT PURSUIT CHANGES YOUR DESIRES, MOTIVES, INTENTIONS, THOUGHTS, ACTIONS AND REACTIONS.

RECORD YOUR EXPERIENCES BELOW:

_____

_____

_____

_____

_____

_____

_____

_____

_____

CHAPTER SIX DECREE:

 I DECREE AND DECLARE THAT MY PURSUIT OF GOD WILL BE EVER INCREASING. I'LL SEE THE GLORY OF GOD AND EXPERIENCE THE REWARD OF LIVING A LIFE OF PURSUIT. NO PART OF MY BEING WILL BE EXEMPT FROM THE ALL OUT PURSUIT, IN JESUS NAME!

CHAPTER SEVEN DISCUSSION

Closing Thoughts

1) WHAT IS THE DIFFERENCE BETWEEN HAVING THE *THOUGHT OF GOD* IN YOUR LIFE VS *THE REALITY OF GOD* IN YOUR LIFE?

_____

_____

_____

_____

_____

_____

2) THE CHAPTER MENTIONS CONVENIENCE. HOW CAN *"CONVENIENCE"* POISON OUR CHRISTIANITY?

_____

_____

_____

_____

_____

_____

3) IN WHAT WAYS HAS *MYSTICAL PRAYER* INSPIRED YOUR DAILY COMMUNION WITH THE LORD? HOW HAVE THE TRUTHS IN THIS BOOK ALTERED YOUR OUTLOOK ON EXPERIENCING GOD?

_____

_____

_____

_____

_____

_____

MYSTICAL CHALLENGE:

BE ENCOURAGED TO LEAVE BEHIND DRY & DEAD RELIGIOUS PRAYING AND STEP INTO THE UNENDING, SUPERNATURAL WORLD OF MYSTICAL PRAYER. AS YOU DO, TAKE NOTE OF THE AUTHENTIC RESULTS IN YOUR MIDST.

RECORD YOUR EXPERIENCES BELOW:

_____

_____

_____

_____

_____

_____

_____

_____

_____

CHAPTER SEVEN DECREE:

 I DECREE AND DECLARE THAT MY PRAYER LIFE WILL BE NOTHING SHORT OF MYSTICAL AND EXPERIENTIAL FROM THIS POINT FORWARD. THE TRUTHS OF THIS WORK WILL SHAKE AND SHAPE MY PRAYER LIFE IN AN IRREVERSIBLE WAY. MAY THIS NEW FOUND FIXATION BE CONTAGIOUS TO ALL WHO COME INTO MY MIDST, IN JESUS NAME!

ABOUT THE AUTHOR

Charlie Shamp is the Co-Founder and President of Destiny Encounters International. He is a sought after international key note speaker. He has been commissioned by Heaven as a Prophet to bring healing and revival in the nations. He has ministered both nationally and internationally with radical demonstrations of faith seeing lives transformed through the power of the Holy Spirit.

Prophet Charlie has predicted major world events with pinpoint accuracy. These include presidential elections, catastrophic natural disasters, revealing government corruptions and exposing terrorism plots. Charlie has been uniquely gifted by God to see and speak accurately into the spirit realm coupled with a ministry of miracles, signs and wonders releasing transformation into churches and cultures worldwide. Through God's divine gifting, Charlie has been given the ability to see the prophetic potential in people and motivate them to cultivate the gifts and talents that often lie dormant within them. He uses the word of God and the power of the prophetic to unearth the hidden treasure God has placed in the believer revealing Heaven's divine plan for their individual lives.

Through the Holy Spirit, God has used Charlie to motivate many to move beyond mediocrity and embrace excellence and greatness. Charlie's heart is to empower and equip the Body of Christ with supernatural insight regarding what God has to say about their destiny and to advance the Kingdom of God in the Earth. People all over the world have been brought to the sacred truth that in Christ they are no longer victims, but overcomers in this life through his ministry.

FOR INFORMATION AND RESOURCES ON THE MINISTRY OF CHARLIE SHAMP VISIT:

DESTINYENCOUNTERS.COM

f facebook.com/charliebrynnshamp

🐦 twitter.com/charlesshamp

📷 instagram.com/charlieshamp

Made in United States
North Haven, CT
28 December 2023

46685751R00083